A Woman's Guide:
30 Days To A Better Mind, Body And Spirit

To Dan

Be well. I think
you for all you do
for others in the area
of wellness — we will
work together again

Shawn Green
20 07

# A Woman's Guide:
# 30 Days To A Better Mind,
# Body And Spirit

Starr Carson-Cleary

The exercises and nutritional advice in A Woman's Guide.... 30 Days to a Better Mind, Body and Spirit is not intended to replace the services of your doctor or to provide an alternative to professional medical advice or treatment, nor does it offer diagnosis of treatment for any specific medical problems. Use this book as a reference guide- it is not meant to be used as a medical manual or guide for self-treatment. Keep in mind that nutritional and physical fitness needs vary from person to person, depending on age, sex, health status, and diet. When it is suggested that you try certain exercises, do so at your own risk, while considering your own physical capabilities. The mind and body exercises demonstrated in this book are extremely gentle movements and should, if carried out as described, be beneficial to your over-all physical and mental well being. All exercises demonstrated in this book are geared to enhancing your strength, flexibility, and muscle endurance. The information in this book is intended to help you make informed decisions about your diet and fitness program.

ISBN : 1-4196-1357-X

To order additional copies, please contact us.
BookSurge, LLC
www.booksurge.com
1-866-308-6235
orders@booksurge.com

# A Woman's Guide:
## 30 Days To A Better Mind, Body And Spirit

# TABLE OF CONTENTS

## PART III - THE MIND AND BODY FITNESS CONNECTION

## PART IV - NUTRITION FACTS - TIPS & BITS

## PART V- WEIGHT LOSS

# Acknowledgements

This project became a reality out of a need to create a universal awareness for women who want to know or reacquaint themselves with their most important assets - their minds, bodies, and spirits. I am grateful to my friends and clients, whose positive health and fitness experiences I have drawn from have helped shape the direction of this book.

Special thanks to my husband Joseph, who has always been supportive and had faith in my ability to go out and spread the message about health and wellness to the masses.

To my baby sister, LaDorsia (Ms Dee), who has taught me so much about life and helped me keep things in perspective, making me laugh until I have cried, when I have felt overwhelmed. To Rex Klein Photography, who took such fabulous photos and made me shine. To Carolyn Hill, who used her precious time off of work and her vacations to help me bring this book to its full manifestation. To Pene, for creating a great, professional looking cover and using my photos to create a great gallery to correspond with the text. And to Don and Pene, husband and wife, who helped me tie it all together by making sure that all the electronic files were set to go without complications.

And to all of you who have encouraged me to continue to write (you know who you are), and those who gave input to help make this project a reality.

Most importantly...to you, the reader, who has taken the time to make the decision to value your most important assets...your mind, body, and spirit. Enjoy the Journey!

# INTRODUCTION

❧

We are all beautiful sisters - we are called Black, White, Red, Yellow, and Brown. I have lived on this planet earth for a long time, and may one day understand why any human being is labeled by the color of their skin, especially when there are few, if any, people in the world with skin colors that are actually White, Black, Red, Brown, or Yellow. The color of our skin varies from shades of rich vanilla cream to dark hot fudge chocolate, with many hues in between.

Although we may live in different parts of the world, we have commonalties in our thinking -fashion, diet, and more than anything, dissatisfaction with our physical appearance. Few of us sister girls are happy with the way our bodies look, we feel that we are either too short, too tall.

Our hips are too wide or too small, or our constant dissatisfaction that the circumference of our waistline is never small enough. We are looking for ways to diminish what we consider flaws in our appearances by using garment body slimmers or enhancements - cosmetics or going to extremes by having plastic surgery. Some of us may feel that our lips are too thin or too large, so we search for the best and latest cosmetic techniques, or medical technology to have them plumped up with injections of Collagen, Botox to freeze frame age lines or make-up tricks to diminish their size. Then... there are the legs that are either too short or chubby, or long and not shapely enough. Our ankles are too fat, too skinny, our eyes too far apart or too close together....

We may be overweight or underweight, going out of our minds trying to emulate the latest fashion and diet craze. The sad fact is that few women diet for health reasons, most diet for aesthetic reasons. Dieting means different things to different people, but it usually means a reduction in the intake of calories for the purpose of losing weight. Some of the weight loss methods range from drastic gastro-intestinal surgery, meal replacement shakes, fruit diets, to all-out fasting.

The way society worships and glamorizes the firm; toned body is seen as representative of a level of success. If you are slender and all of your curves are located in the right areas on your body than, slenderness represents power, energy and control. Being slender has generally been associated with happiness, success and social acceptability, while the overweight person is often seen as unattractive, lazy, lacking willpower, and out of control. All you have to do is look around daily and see that most women are not slim, nor do they have toned bodies, and most of them do not wear a size 4, size 6, or even a size 8. (The last time I checked, the average dress size for women is a size 14.)

Although some of us sister girls will not admit it, there are still women in the world on a continuous mission to keep up with society's current ideology of how the perfect woman should look. I have a firm belief in keeping the body in tip-top form, internally and externally, so if you decide on a bit of body transformation, tummy tuck, breast enlargement, liposuction, facelift or brow lift – hopefully your motives for making these physical changes are clearly defined. Are you making a change to your body because you are trying to fit into a mold set by society's criteria? On the other hand, are you making physical changes that will not only enhance your appearance, but will also give you a feeling of satisfaction from the inside out? You must decide.

No matter what we look like, we are all unique and beautiful in our own way - strong women of all shapes and sizes. Remember that beauty is only skin deep, and comes from the inside to outside. You may be familiar with the saying "beauty is only skin deep, but ugly goes as deep as the bone".

**A Woman's Guide…"3O Days To A Better Mind, Body, and Spirit "** is not a book about the latest popular liquid diet, low carbohydrate diet, fitness trend, or mind-altering technique. It is about getting in touch with the person who resides within her own skin, her personal power, and a complete health and wellness lifestyle change.

The starting process of mind, body, and spirit transformation begins progressively with a major physical and mental overhaul. In order to begin to accomplish such a feat, you will need to do a little research on yourself. This exercise is divided into two parts.

Part one is more crucial than part two because you will need to look deep down within yourself to do some soul searching. First, I am going to ask you from this point on, look deep down within yourself and begin to examine just what you would like to achieve in creating a new and improved you.

Part two requires you to stand in front of your mirror for three to five minutes and make mental observations about your body. (If you really want to do some soul searching, try this exercise fully undressed.) Do you like what you see? What can you do to improve your posture, your over-all physical appearance? After making a few observations, ask yourself if the changes you plan to make are realistic, or are you dealing with genetics that cannot be changed? Try to be as honest as possible in your assessment, and use it as a starting point to improve your body. Follow me on this journey to create a feeling of maximum well being and develop a vibrant, energetic, yet peaceful individual who not only knows and understands who she is, but accepts, embraces, and idolizes the body, mind, and spirit that the Creator has bestowed upon her.

This book has been written not only for women who feel that their mind, body, and spirit is in need of recharging, an awakening, or total enlightenment, but also for the men in their lives who are interested in learning and gaining a better understanding about their mother's, wife's, and daughter's well being.

I wish you happiness, peace of mind, serenity, and a lifetime of good health and wellness.

Starr

*I dedicate A Woman's Guide...30 Days to a Better Mind, Body and Spirit to four of my best friends: Colette, Debs, Sally and Viola.*

*Friends are wonderful: best friends are like sisters. Friends give inspiration and encouragement, and cheer each other along the way. Our friends can be as diverse and infinite as the adjectives we choose to describe them - friends in a real sense, reflect the choices we make in life.*

*Like any kind of relationship, friends can be lost within our lifetime. People come into our lives and people leave - but fond memories last forever. Treasure the memories.*

*"If you want to keep a friendship alive, the effort has to be made between friends" to keep it long lasting.*

# PART I

## *YOUR BODY*

❧

## THE RAT RACE

Living in our fast-paced society, we have too many obligations and commitments to keep in shorter spans of time. Our lives are crammed with chores, to-do lists, and more. Our home life, work, and other unexpected events throughout the day contribute to make us feel stressed. From the time we open our eyes in the morning, most of us hit the ground running on a daily basis...school lunches need to be made, the children need to be driven to school. Then there are the extra curriculum school activities; soccer for one child, baseball for another and yet another child opts for volleyball or cheerleading practice. Let's not forget there are meals that need to be prepared in the evening, homework to be checked and other chores that must be done before ending your day.

We have all become multi-task jugglers. We are mothers, sisters, wives, aunts, and grandmothers, who are often the head of the household. If we are not helping the children with school projects and homework, we are organizing or attending fundraisers for the kids, our workplace, or a charity. If we are parents, we are trying to give undivided attention, guidance, and structure to each and every one of our offspring. We become coaches because we want to be involved in our children's extra curriculum activities, or we become social secretaries in charge of birthday parties, vacations, friend and family get-togethers etc.

The weekly grocery list has been tucked under a magnet on the refrigerator for two weeks. Your to-do list continues to grow daily because you can't seem to find enough time in your day to shop for everything you need in one trip. Instead, every other day you stop at the grocery store and pick up a few items at a time. You put your dry cleaning in your car on Monday, chauffeur it around all week, and realize at 3:00 am on Saturday morning that you forgot to go to the cleaners. Now you have two problems; the dry cleaner is closed until Monday, and you have few clothing options for the upcoming week...more stress. You haven't balanced your checkbook in a while because you either have no time to do it or no money in the account (or both), and you still have a week to go before you get paid again.

If it's not the daily commute to work, there is the pressure of getting to work on time and performing your job, going to business meetings, school activities, other family activities and running errands at an optimum pace. All the while the merry-go-round of life seems to go faster every day.

Ladies, let's face it, you may or may not admit it - but you are true magicians when it comes to managing all the activities in your daily life. Many of us accomplish more things in one day than some people accomplish in two or three days. Whether we are single or married, or a single parent, our days are busy from morning until night. If we are single, we may have a different lifestyle than the married couple or the part-time parent who shares the child rearing with a spouse on alternate schedules. Nonetheless, the days seem to get shorter while our to-do list continues to grow longer.

Some of us live for the weekend because we know it will be the only chance we get to catch our breath to regroup before starting a new week. However, the weekend has finally arrived...you have planned a quiet weekend to catch-up on some much needed rest, maybe even give yourself a day of pampering - facial, pedicure, and a long soak in a hot bubble bath. All of that changes shortly. The kids have other plans for the weekend - they have invited a few of their friends for a sleepover at your house! There goes your quiet weekend.

Now you have twenty minutes to yourself before you hit the ground running to play hostess mom for your young houseguests. "Oh well," you tell yourself "...there is always next weekend." But you know that next weekend, and the one after that will probably be a repeat of the last few weekends. Busy.

Because our lives are so hectic, a large percentage of sister girls are going to doctors and therapists in record numbers for depression, anxiety, and bouts of memory loss. The statistics are astonishing on the number of prescriptions written for women for depression, anxiety, and panic attacks. Women often tell me that they have no time to relax and catch their breath; some have taken drastic measures and resorted to Prozac, Paxil, Zoloft, and other anti-depressants. Something has to give...and someone has to make a concerted effort to make time for the most important person in your life...You!

If you hit the ground running every day without taking time for yourself, or if you are just floating through life existing from one day to the next without taking time out for yourself.

***It's time to make a change in your life!***


## *OUR SACRED VESSEL...OUR BODY*


Let's talk about the house you currently reside in...your body. Your body houses life's experiences on all levels: physical, emotional, and spiritual. Positive, loving successful experiences help create, and free our physical movements, while undesirable memories, physical and mental traumas (self imposed or inflicted by others), stress, and suppressed emotions harm our spiritual, as well as physical beings. Negativity affects every cell of our body, possibly leading to the derailment of our hopes and dreams.

Ever notice how our minds may choose not to remember past traumas, but our bodies never forget or deny the past? The human body is a divinely created machine and should be treated with the reverence and respect you give other important aspects in your life.

## *OUR BODY CLEANSING MACHINE*

Do you wake up some mornings feeling tired and parts of your body aching with nagging pain? Do you often lack the energy to get out of bed in the morning? Do you experience constipation on a regular basis? Do you need alcohol, caffeine, sugar, or other substances to get through the day? If you answer yes to one or more of these questions, you may be a candidate for body cleansing. The first stage to creating a healthier, more radiant new you is to cleanse the body and mind while purifying the spirit.

Every day our bodies are subjected to toxins in many forms: plastics, solvents, the poisons in the moisturizers and the make-up we apply to our skin, even the hair coloring we use to enhance our locks. Enter any nail salon and your nasal passages will probably go into orbit from the smell of the acrylic substances being used to glamorize our short finger nails into one or two-inch works of art. These are only some of the topical toxins we interact with on a regular basis.

Let's face it – the subject of additives is still a highly controversial subject, but most of the precooked foods we eat contain additives, flavor enhancers, cooking agents, etc. Even though additives are added to protect us from food spoilage and prolong the shelf life of items, these conveniences may have a downside. The human body must assimilate and then break down the chemicals in the additives so the body can try to process them. It is vital to create a balance in selecting the foods you eat. Eat as many wholesome meals as possible, and as few processed foods as possible.

Because of all of the toxins that are so prevalent, we need to eliminate the toxicity from our bodies as frequently as possible. All of the toxins we ingest orally or topically eventually make their way into our intestines. If we do not have a good, strong constitution, or if our elimination organs are blocked or functioning poorly, the toxins may be reabsorbed right back into the body in a more concentrated form, and at a much faster rate. The reabsorption back into the body will make you feel sick, and could possibly be fatal. As our bodies play host to the buildup of toxins, we may suffer from headaches, anger, frustration, puffiness, bloating and digestive problems, often indicators that something is very wrong internally.

## *WHAT IS BODY CLEANSING?*

After a long winter season of cold and dreary weather, and being confined in our homes behind closed doors and windows for months, most of us get the urge to start a major endeavor: spring-cleaning. We begin turning things upside down, moving furniture, dusting, purging, building and renovating. Window coverings are removed from windows, and heavy bedding is exchanged for lighter weight fabrics. Colors are changed from dark drab to vibrant and cheerful. Cabinets are emptied and the contents replaced with new, or fewer items…all because we want to have a clean, fresh new look in our homes.

Occasionally our bodies need a thorough cleansing. Some of us frequently eat fried foods, high fat snacks, processed foods, synthetic foods, and foods with preservatives. As we take prescription and over the counter drugs, abuse our bodies with stimulants, sedatives, and alcohol, our health continues to deteriorate at an alarming rate. Further indications of the body being in need of detoxification includes poor digestion, bloating, constipation and bowel irregularity, mood changes, raised blood pressure, water retention, decreased tolerance of fatty foods and alcohol, profuse sweating, and unpleasant body odor.

A woman's body can play host to many toxins that may contribute to puffiness, bloating, digestive problems, etc. Body cleansing aids in ridding the body of toxins by enhancing the body's own natural cleansing process, and the results are usually phenomenal.

## *RELEASING TOXINS THROUGH BODY DETOXIFICATION*

Body cleansing, or detoxification, reduces toxin buildup and improves the elimination systems of the body (the liver, the digestive system, the skin, and the kidneys). The liver is one of the body's most valuable organs. The sole function of the liver is to cleanse the blood in the body so the other organs of the body can be nourished by purified blood, while neutralizing toxic waste and sending it off to the kidneys and the intestines for elimination. The digestive system is one of the body's first defense mechanisms. It works by breaking foods down to release essential nutrients, and then absorbing and discharging waste from the body. Here are a few reasons for cleansing the body:

*   Body purification

*   Clearer skin

*   Disease prevention

*   Gives internal organs a rest and time to heal from system overload

*   Rejuvenation

*   Slows the aging process

*   Weight loss

Most people do not realize that the skin is the largest organ of the body. Like the liver, it is another detoxifying organ that is responsible for the excretion of waste materials through the skin's pores. Manifestation of these toxins will appear on your face, hair, nails, and other parts of your body in the form of blemishes, wrinkles, and acne. Once the liver becomes overloaded, the toxins in your body find their way to your skin. Your hair can become dull and lifeless, and your nails may turn yellow, split easily, and develop white spots.

This is your body letting you know that it is deficient in specific vitamins and nutrients. For instance, vitamin A works as a wrinkle fighter, Vitamin B, a stress and duress buffer, Vitamin C, the collagen builder, and Vitamin E works as an antioxidant by keeping free radicals away. All of these components are needed in ridding environmental toxins from the body. In recent years, more and more doctors have recommended the use of saunas and exercise to help the body eliminate toxins. The result produces a healthy glow to the skin, and often the skin looks younger.

The kidney's main function is to filter the blood and remove toxins from the body. The kidneys work best when we drink plenty of water, and when we periodically cleanse the body. The body purification process is vital for releasing toxins, because without it, the body actually begins to age prematurely.

## WHY YOU SHOULD USE A BODY CLEANSING PROGRAM

We cleanse the body for health, vitality, and rejuvenation. A detoxification or body-cleansing program can help treat disease and possibly prevent future health problems. The reason our bodies become overloaded with toxins is usually due to the rapid pace of our busy lifestyles, and poor diets deficient of the nutrients, vitamins, and minerals the body needs to perform the natural detoxification functions well.

## WHO SHOULD CLEANSE THEIR BODY?

Everyone should cleanse his or her body. Some people need to cleanse continually to keep their bodies in balance along with good nutrition and maintenance. If your regular diet is balanced and void of excesses of food, alcohol, and other evil food temptations, then the detoxification process should be less intense. Anyone can cleanse their body, but the need may be greater for those who:

• Abuse alcohol

• Are overweight and tend to over-eat

• Eat fatty and/or sweet foods

- Eat poorly balanced diets

- Fatigue easily

- Frequently use over the counter, prescription, or recreational drugs

- Have food or environmental allergies

- Regularly consume fast foods

- Smoke

- Suffers from nose and throat congestion

- use caffeine, sugar, or other substances

## WHAT ARE THE BEST BODY CLEASING PROGRAMS?

The answer to this question is a personal preference. Some of the most popular cleanses are herbal cleanses, broth, cascara sarsara, colon cleanses, fruit juice cleanses (apple, berry, pineapple), and fasting. Cleansing programs are designed primarily to rid the body of accumulated toxins and poisons. Accumulated toxins like drug residues, insecticides, pesticides, heavy metals, and even radioactive materials can be flushed from fat cells and other tissues through a viable detoxification program.

## HOW LONG SHOULD A CLEANSING PROGRAM LAST?

Depending on what your time schedule will allow, you should decide what would work best for your needs. There are 3O day first-time detoxification programs that are mild enough to start on a weekend, that taper off enough so you can function through the week without feeling like you have to go to the ladies room every twenty minutes. There are also rebalancing and cleansing programs that are perfect for busy schedules, and mini-fasts that work great in two days.

## WHEN SHOULD YOU BEGIN A CLEANSING PROGRAM?

I always suggest starting any cleansing or body detoxification program at a time when you can maintain a routine schedule. Most people have no problem starting a detoxification program any day of the week. However, if you have never used a cleansing product, you might want to consider starting a program when you have a few days at home. Try to start your cleansing program on a Friday, especially if this is your first time on a detoxification program. The first few days are usually the hardest.

Note: 3O days before starting a detoxification program try to:

- Avoid or minimize red meats, organ meats, refined foods, canned foods, sugar, salt, saturated fats, alcohol, nicotine, over the counter and prescription drugs if at all possible

- Drink plenty of water

- Eat foods that are more organic

- Include fruits, vegetables, grains, legumes, nuts, fresh fish, and organic poultry in your diet

- Remember to always consult your doctor before starting a detoxification program

As you complete the body cleansing process, you will began to value your body more as a temple than as a mobile shell that carries you from place to place. As your body begins to release the cumulative tensions from the past, you will began to experience mindfulness - living in the present moment while experiencing gradual surges of freedom, vitality, and last, but most important, your power!

## MENTAL CLEANSING

Cleansing the mind is as important as cleansing the body. Once you begin to clear mental, emotional, and spiritual blocks, your anxiety and other negative feelings will dissipate and be replaced with peacefulness, serenity and happiness. The choice is up to you to have an abundance of physical energy, time to relax and be mentally calm, and enjoy the freedom of choice that comes from over-all well being.

Every year, statistics indicate we are living longer. We may be living longer, have all the modern conveniences at our disposal that helps us save time, and yet, how much time have we really gained? Sure, we are fortunate to get our daily chores done faster, but then we try to cram in a few more things before we feel we can call it a day. The quality of life is just as important as the quantity of time we live. What good does it do for any of us to work hard to purchase material things we want, yet have no time to enjoy them?

Stress is a familiar word to all of us. Our world is moving faster and faster and we want to have fun and excitement. It is also challenging, trying, and demanding, because we want to accomplish many things within a certain time period. As we try to time manage every single minute of the day, we often find ourselves in a stress-related turmoil of anxiety, worry, and anticipation. Our bodies and minds can only tolerate so much. After a while, the body reaches the saturation point resulting in system overload, becoming uncomfortable, unbearable, or even intolerable.

Once we start feeling overloaded and overwhelmed, we need to find a way to relax, but there is no magic pill to help eliminate these feelings. However, there are choices that can be made in life that will not slow the world down, but will certainly help us all cope better. There is a way to neutralize the feeling of being on a fast moving merry-go-round and overwhelmed. We do not have to continue to live in the fast lane, moving from one experience to another without time for reflection. If we cannot learn from our life experiences, what have we accomplished?

You and I are works in progress; unique individuals that need to have emotional and spiritual debris brushed away, one layer at a time. After all, some of the emotional debris may have been stored within your body for weeks, months, or even years. You will begin to understand the statement "taking back your power", as you come to the realization that your empowerment and personal drive to pursue your dreams and make them come true becomes a reality.

Slowing down our daily hectic pace is a hard thing to do, especially for most women. As multi-taskers, we usually contemplate what our next task will be before we have accomplished our current one. So, how about slowing down and finding some quiet time for yourself? At this moment you are probably thinking to yourself "I barely have time to go to the ladies room, take a lunch break, or actually eat lunch instead of running errands during my lunch hour!"

I know it is almost impossible to find time for yourself, but the sanity you save may be your own. If you don't learn to take a short timeout for yourself regularly, you are not only cheating yourself out of an opportunity to mentally regroup, but also positive interaction with people you may come into contact with. It can make a big difference in how you handle difficult situations. It takes a lot of practice to get out of the fast lane, but it can be mastered if you create short intervals of quiet time for yourself.

What can you do in this short, quiet time? You can meditate. Many of us have dabbled in meditation through conscious relaxation and didn't realize we were doing it. Maybe you have experienced the inner reflection of meditation during an exercise class, while managing pain (perhaps at the dentist's office), or in a quiet moment before taking a test.

You may need to start with a short, five to ten minute timeout, and gradually increase the time by longer increments, until you can take a three day weekend, or a weeklong retreat. Whatever you do, start to take time for yourself. You will feel better about things and may even find that you are less stressed, and most importantly, you will be a delightful person to be around.

## *RELAXING THROUGH MEDITATION*

If you looking for a way to find inner peace while calming your mind, body, and spirit, you will find comfort in the practice of meditation. The practical effort of meditation is to completely focus on breathing, remove the 'clutter' that constantly tries to invade the mind, and eliminate any feelings that would hinder calmness. The repeated goal of meditation is to clear the mind - to think of nothing. This form of getting in touch with your peacefulness is often called 'meditation through relaxation' or 'chosen relaxation', because the working goal is to reach a state of serenity. Meditation can offer peace, serenity, calmness, lead to new insights, and is actually easier to do than you might imagine.

**Selecting Your Meditation Space:**

• Find a quiet place where you will be able to relax without interruptions, clear your mind, and focus on your breathing

• Use a comfortable setting for your meditation

• You may want to sit in a comfortable chair or sit on a soft pillow

• You may light candles or incense if you choose

• You may prefer silence, or you may want to turn on soft, soothing music or chimes

• Set a timer, if you have a limited time to meditate

Each of us will find that we have our own unique path to peace, relaxation, and spiritual healing. I cannot give you a timeline for finding inner peace, but I can offer guidance on your journey of soul searching to find the peace and serenity that you desire.

Once you begin the mind and body cleansings and become more in tune with every aspect of your body, relaxation and the release of tight and inflexible muscles will come with minimal effort. You will find that the process of unwinding from a busy day gets easier and becomes second nature.

## *EXERCISE AND YOUR BODY*

**No body is perfect.** Whatever your age, race or gender, we all fall within the category of a body type. All of us have inherited body prototypes through genetics. Every man and woman is a mixture of body type characteristics. William Sheldon, a psychologist and

Researcher, discovered the history of body typing. Sheldon was so fascinated with the theory of prototypes that he dedicated most of his life, even has a child observing animals and birds. Later in life, he turned his hobby into observing the characteristics of the human body. There are three basic body types: Ectomorph (Ecto), Mesomorph (Meso), and Endomorph (Endo). Sheldon quickly grasped the concept that although a person's body type may consist of one, two or even all three-body types, one body type usually dominates over the other two.

This is why it is important to know what your specific body type is, in order to determine which exercise program will work best for you to produce maximum results. I believe that everyone has the potential to develop a great physical shape regardless of his or her body type- if they are aware which body type is most dominate.

The biggest mistake a lot of women make when they are trying to make positive changes to their body is to strive to physically look like another person. Sometimes we forget that there are certain aspects of our bodies that cannot be changed unless they are surgically enhanced.
Case in point -a woman genetically may come from a family where all of the women have, short legs, thick ankles, small waistlines and ample hips. There is no diet plan in the world that will help her to lose enough weigh to get slender ankles, and smaller hips, But if she learns which body type is most dominate in her lineage, she will be able to identify and work on a fitness plan that will help to put less emphasis on those parts of body while sculpting and toning other areas to accentuate the positive.

Since most people exhibit a predominance of one body type, with aspects of the other two. Your dominant body type will be the one you focus on when establishing a fitness program for yourself. If you are not sure what your body type is, or which exercise program will work best for you, I have given you a synopsis of each body type, and a brief description of the recommended exercises for each. See if you recognize the physical characteristics of your body type:

**Ectomorph** body types (my secondary body type) are usually long and rectangular (beanpole shaped), lightly muscled slender in the shoulders, waist and hips. Ectomorph body types are considered lucky by some people, because they have more of an angular appearance, often have fast metabolisms, and do not gain weight easily. When this body type does gain weight, the weight tends to be distributed evenly over the entire body. Because of their lack of shape and low muscle weight, the lean muscle weight is what helps define and give the body its shapely physique. The best exercise for female Ectomorph body types includes aggressive strength training without gaining lots of muscle mass. Men with this body type will benefit the most by training with heavier weights – helps to gain larger muscle size.

**Mesomorph** body types (my body type) are characterized by broad shoulders, a narrow waist, naturally large muscles, and a fast metabolism due to the amount of lean muscle mass. This body type is often called 'gifted' because they are genetically predisposed to great muscular gains. Mesomorphs tend to lose fat and build muscle faster than other body types. Thirty-minute sessions of cardiovascular exercises are recommended 2 to 3 times a week, but Mesomorph types should use caution when training. It is important to give the muscles time to rest between workouts. Working too long or too frequently will cause muscle fatigue and loss of muscle mass. Since this body type gains muscle very easily, some people would call this the best body type if you were trying to bulk up. Female Mesomorphs who do not want to build heavy muscle should focus on lifting lighter weights, and perform more repetitions increasing you're your sets as you become stronger.

**Endomorph** body types have a tendency to be large boned, stocky and have a slower metabolism. Endomorphs tend to be apple-shaped because they tend to gain weight mainly in the abdomen. Their legs are shorter than their torso, and their chests tend to be larger than average person's. This body type may have a smaller bone structure, and gains weight easily. Recommended exercises for this body type are fitness moves that help enhance the metabolism. Circuit training, supersets, aerobic exercises- swimming, jogging/powerwalking and biking. Periodic strength training will help burn more calories. Using heavy weights that will limit the total amount of repetitions performed is not recommended. My best recommendation is to perform several repetitions using moderate weights and short pauses between sets.

As I mentioned earlier, there are very few people in the world with perfect Ecto, Meso, or Endo body types. Most of our body types usually fall somewhere in between the characteristics of Ectomorph, Mesomorphs and Endomorphs. To create an effective and successful fitness program, it is essential to become familiar with your own body type.

Achieving the **'Perfect Body'** is an attainable goal, but not a realistic one. It is difficult, if not impossible; to change the body you genetically inherited from your parents. Work with the body type you have. Learn as much as you can about good nutrition and fitness for your specific body type. Exercise at least 3 to 5 times a week to lose or to maintain weight loss.
Just remember...

'NO BODY IS PERFECT!

Creating a customized weight management and fitness plan is an individual venture. If you have correctly identified your body type, you have won half of the weight loss battle because you can now start on a correct wellness program. Whatever you decide to do in your fitness or weight loss endeavors- stay consistent!

## *A FEW WORDS FOR OUR PLUS SIZE SISTERS*

Here are a Few Startling Statistics to digest:

Nearly two thirds of United States adults are over weight, which also includes those who are obese.

- Over Weight Adults: (Body Mass Index 25 percent)

- Adults 20 years or older- 129.6 million (64.5 percent)

- Women 20 years or older- 64.5 million (61.9 percent)

- Men 20 years or older 65.1 million (96.2 percent)

- Obese Adults (Body Mass Index 30)

- Nearly one-third of United States adults are obese (BMI 30 percent)

- 300,000 deaths occur every year in the United States are associated with obesity.

- Overweight and obesity are associated with heart disease, some types of cancer, type 2 diabetes, stroke, breathing problems and depression.

- Less than one-third of United States adults get regular leisure-time physical activity- five times or more per week for 30 minutes or more each time or robust activities three times or more for 20 minutes or more each time. About 10 percent of adults do no physical activity at all.

There is not a day that goes by, that someone in the public is talking about how overweight the American population has become. It seems that daily necessity items are customized more and more to accommodate our plus size figures. Weather you are listening to the radio, watching television on discussing the topic about **"The War on Obesity"**, it seems that a large percentage of Americans are either overweight or obese. The casualties include men, women and the next generation – our children of all ages.

Sometimes I get the feeling that some people in the world have become either oblivious about their ample sizes or they are in total denial. The Plus Size Sister or brother for that matter should not have to bear all of the blame. From birth, diapers are made larger for the ample size baby bottom and baby car seats and strollers are being manufactured in larger sizes. This is only the starting point. Movie theatre seats, doctors' examination tables, beds are made stronger with reinforcement to accommodate larger body frames, chairs are built larger without arms to prevent embarrassing moments –like remaining attached to the person once they try to stand up. Airline seats are made wider. Even emergency vehicles are using power lifts that will lift patients up to 800 pounds, while preventing injuries to staff members. I guess you could say lastly- even the casket makers are joining the marketing trends- even at the end of life; the final resting bed has even been designed to give the dearly departed- extra space.

If you are overweight, you probably do not want to be reminded daily that our society is heading more toward plus size intolerance. I'm sure you know it all too well. The airline industry wants you to purchase an additional seat instead of one. If you cannot pass the one-seat criteria: you must be able to sit in the chair without your girth spilling over into the next chair or aisle and you must be able to close the seat beat around you're your body. You are probably apprehensive about going to a movie theatre, because the space between the rows in the theatre are too narrow and you don't want to embarrass yourself by not being able to fit, so you sit at home and view movies in your private domain. The clothing industry wants you to shop at specialty clothing stores (You know this well, because you cannot find your dress size on the rack at your favorite store at the mall.)

I have been told by some plus size people; that their anxiety level goes up a few decimals every time they have to interact with the outside world, because they have to emotionally plan a strategy by analyzing the upcoming task. Questions that often plague the plus size person include- will there be table and chairs at the restaurant as well as booths? If so are the chairs sturdy enough to contain my frame? Are the bathroom stalls large enough to hold my plus size frame? How many people will look at me with disgust or pity- worst yet, how many will look right through me as if I were invisible? It really takes a psychologically toll on a person, when they are constantly being reminded that they are taking up too much space and utilizing too many resources that accommodate the plus size individual.

Sure, some of the main causes of being overweight stem from eating more food than the body requires, and lack of voluntary physical exercise. But their may also be others factors- poor dietary habits, yoyo dieting, slow metabolism, genetics, medical conditions etc. Instead of offering support, the pressure that society is putting on plus size people is creating an adverse reaction. I have also been told by some of my clients, that all the coverage about being overweight- and the special circumstance penalties that have been imposed on the plus size person has contributed to more self-hate of their bodies, and has made it harder for them to eat and live a healthier lifestyle.

I have extra compassion-NOT pity, when I see a plus size person-; there is a difference between the two. I don't feel sorry for the person, but try to put myself in their shoes. I wonder if the person is a victim of the many promises of miracle diets or exercise equipment gadgetry. Have they given up on trying to manage their weight, be functional fit or have they resolved themselves to being overweight, immobile and life in a state of hopelessness.

I wanted to add this chapter, because I want to continue to emphasize and stress the importance of improving your health through fitness and positive dietary changes, no matter how overweight you might be, how wide your waistline is or how large your clothing size may be.

Lets talk about the big picture. First- lets focus on eating healthier and finding fitness movements that will work for your individual physical capabilities. There is much more to being in shape, than have a twenty five-inch waistline. You do not have to be thin or look like a professional model to be healthy. Remember looks can be deceiving. Just because a person is thin is no guarantee that they are the epitome of perfect health.

"My hope and dream will one day become a reality – That we as a sisterhood will one day truly understand that you do not have to wear a single number digit dress size to be healthy." Until that day comes, I believe that we will continue to pass the mentally on to every generation, that you are not attractive unless you fit into the current fashion size mode.

To some being fit means being able to run marathon or bench press several pounds of free weights, to others it might mean, waking every morning with a great sense of wellness. What ever your definition of being fit, you will need to integrate a few fitness components to make sure that you have a well-rounded and balanced fitness program.

Okay, "No more excuses"- there are exercises that everyone can do- as long as you are able to move your body parts, you can build strength, increase your cardio activity, flexibility, muscular strength and your endurance. Consider the areas that you are stronger or areas that you may lack strength, flexibility, muscle endurance, or aerobic endurance. Make a long term plan to improve in each of your lackluster areas. The human body was designed for physical activity; although we sit, slouch, bend, lift and carry things, and sit at our desks and rise many times during the day, it is not enough movement to get or maintain or keep our muscles in top condition.

I want you to know that the most important thing for you is to get moving, one step at a time. As I mentioned earlier, there are physical movements that you can to do to get yourself started on a fitness routine.

**Some of these subtle gradual changes in your life will improve your:**

- Cardiovascular Health

- Flexibility

- Balance and Coordination

- Blood Circulation

- Energy and Stamina

- Self Esteem

- Functional Mobility

I want you to focus on what you want your body to accomplish physically- and ask yourself a few serious questions. This is not a test. Your answers will help to determine how functionally fit you are and give you a starting point for staring an exercise regiment.

- Can you currently get yourself off of the floor without assistance if you were to fall?

- Is it a major effort for you to get in and out of your vehicle?

- Do you fear going to places that may have steps or where you may need to walk a short distance on an incline?

- When go to a public place, do you feel anxiety, because you are not sure if you can fit into a chair, the ladies room, stand for long periods of time or you fear that people will either stare at you or pretend that you are invisible.

- Do you have difficulty bending down to put on your socks, shoes, lacing up your shoes?

- Feel discouraged that the only clothing you can wear is spandex.

- Do you have than five dress sizes in your clothes closet-purchased within the last two years?

If you answered yes to three or more of these questions, you may be heading into the danger zone of obesity and poor health. It is never too late to start a healthy lifestyle. Pace yourself and take one day at a time. Be good to yourself and nourish your body with love and kindness.

The Bottom Lines- In a nutshell, if you are inactivity and you eat more than you have been active, you will gain weight.

If you start moving more, find a fitness activity that you like-you will begin to feel better, eat less, and lose weight.

Forget- the low fat, fat free, no carbohydrate, liquid and yo-yo diets. There is no such thing as a successful diet. The best dietary regiment for losing and maintaining your weight. Eat a balanced sensible diet and maintain a regular exercise schedule.

### *"Empower Yourself Through Movement"*

If you feel like you are carrying a few extra pounds, are overweight or obese, you are not alone. Most overweight people have tried various diets and new exercise techniques with varied success. More than one-half of Americans who say that they are overweight are trying to slim down.

If you are carrying a few extra pounds, are overweight or obese, you may be at risk for developing heart disease, diabetes, cancer, or suffering a stroke. There are many theories on why we are overweight: genetics, medications, menopause, thyroid complications, metabolism etc., but until a new theory comes along that proves to be the absolute answer, we must try to develop a healthy diet plan that works the best for ourselves.

Let's get back to basics. The best way to lose weight, and maintain a healthy weight is by eating healthy, balanced, and proportioned meals, coupled with a regular regiment of exercise. Exercise is the single best tool in the battle to lose weight, and for maintaining a normal body weight. It also provides other tremendous health benefits, including better control of blood pressure, stronger, healthier heart and lungs, and stronger bones.

Exercise can make a dramatic difference in weight control, and adhering to a moderate exercise program is the best defense against being overweight. Exercise builds lean muscles, and when you have more muscle, you burn calories all day long. It's like turning up the volume on your metabolism. Even if you can only walk or jog just a little at a steady speed, you can benefit from a sensible exercise program emphasizing consistency, low intensity, and motivation.

Exercise combined with a low calorie diet, and motivating techniques like fat testing calipers and tracking your progress daily can have a positive impact on your body, while nourishing your spirit as well. And if you walk 15 minutes a day and do not consume more calories than your body needs, you can lose 10 pounds a year!

Overweight and obese people often experience discomfort, pain, or injury early on when exercising to advance to a higher level. Try non-weight-bearing activities such as bicycling and swimming. To improve balance or to help with agility, choose options like walking because it does not take a lot of athletic ability. A person can lose extra pounds by adding more physical activity to their lifestyle, and using any opportunity, such as taking the stairs, walking the distance across a parking lot, or walking to the mailbox will help increase their fitness program.

Aerobic exercise is crucial to any exercise program. Make sure to select a fitness activity you can do for a long period of time. Walking is always my first suggestion for my fitness clients. Jogging is also great (if your knees are in good shape, as it is harder on the knees). If you are not able to jog, but want to walk at a faster pace than your normal gait, try Power Walking. This vigorous movement helps you move faster, increasing your heart rate and improving your circulation, giving your body a full cardiovascular workout that will burn more calories.

If you want to start exercising, but are not sure that your joints can start off with a weight bearing fitness program, select exercises that are non-weight bearing, i.e. swimming. Dancing, cycling, and hiking are also alternative means for fitness fun.

As I work and train overweight and obese clients in private settings, I realize many of them do not want to exercise publicly because they are embarrassed by the way they may look. Most of them do not want to wear leggings or leotards in front of others, or even look at themselves as they pass a window or mirror. It is important to find a place and a time to exercise when one is not self-conscious. The most frequent excuse I hear from clients who are overweight or obese is that they do not feel comfortable enough to go to a traditional gym to take a tour of the facility, much less sign up for a one year membership.

Although I teach worksite fitness and conduct one-on-one fitness training, I have taught exercise classes in health clubs for a number of years. The fitness industry has continued to reinvent itself by offering new programs to entice new members to join their clubs, but there is still room for improvement when it comes to marketing and outreach for plus-size people. I personally would like to see more 'size sensitivity' training, more space between exercise equipment in the workout room, and possibly separate women's classes for plus-size ladies. I say this because many ladies do not feel comfortable working out in a fitness class alongside men. The plus-size person is not asking for special treatment when they join a fitness club. All they need are fitness programs that will help them become functionally fit. Functional fitness training programs strengthen and tone the major muscles of the body which are beneficial for sitting, standing, getting out of a chair, getting down on the floor and up again independently. Being able to do these simple things may mean the difference between a person remaining independent by being mobile, or becoming dependent upon others for their basic needs.

The following is a scenario that I have seen or heard many times from some clients about their first-time health club experience. The client finally makes the decision to take that first step - getting the nerve up to take a tour of a health club facility. In most instances, the staff person is quite friendly, as well as helpful.

As the potential plus-size member tours the facility, usually the first thing the client notices is the lean and tanned models mingling around the gym, who look as if they spend many hours there working out. The glamorous pictures of male and female models on the walls bear no resemblance to their body type. They see fitness machines they know will be next too impossible to fit on (unless they lose 50 or 60 pounds, which is the reason they are at the gym). After being introduced to the personal trainer the client feels intimidated, because the trainer may look as if he or she has never been five pounds over their goal weight.

As the potential client continues to evaluate everything about the facility, things that the average size person may not consider are always on their mind. The plus-size person may not ask the staff member how sturdy the chairs are, but may wonder if the chairs are strong enough to hold their body without collapsing? Are the toilet and shower stalls large enough to accommodate them? Are there other plus-size members? These may be small or non-existent issues for some gym members, but they are very real and often traumatic matters to a plus-size person venturing into these new surroundings.

**If you are a plus-size person, before joining a health club:**

- Choose a club where most of the clientele is NOT pencil thin.

- May sure that your fitness program is right for you.

- See if the club has different types of clientele during the day.

- Is there ample room for you to maneuver between fitness machines with ease?

- Find out if classes are offered for overweight, or a similar plus-size exercise group with which you will feel comfortable, and welcomed.

- Does the health club offer classes on weight loss motivation and nutrition, as well as fitness classes?

- Do the classes change routines often to help keep the class interesting, fun, and motivating?

The name of the game is to not only select a fitness activity you like, but also to find a gym, area of your home or location that is well lighted, and produces a environment that you will be able to frequent on a regular basis. You will continue exercising if it is fun, or pleasing in some other way. For instance, you may like a fitness activity because it is an opportunity to socialize. Walking happens to be an excellent activity for verbal interaction with a friend while trimming your waistline in the process.

According to a recent Centers' for Disease Control survey, the most popular exercises for overweight adults trying to lose weight are:

**Men**
Walking - 37.7%
Running and Jogging - 10.7%
Weight Lifting - 9.6%
Golfing - 8.1%

**Women**
Walking - 52.5%
Aerobics - 8.7%
Gardening - 8.2%
Exercise Machines - 8%

Do not exclude yourself from the wonderful health benefits of exercise. Step up to the plate and take advantage of the many benefits to your health, attitude, and physical appearance that regular exercise can provide.

Always check with your doctor or health specialist before starting a new dietary or fitness program exercise, especially if you are extremely overweight. Surround yourself with people who have positive, healthy lifestyles.

## *SET POINT AND BODY WEIGHT*

Ever wonder what your ideal weight should be? How do you know if you are at your ideal weight? You are probably at your best body weight when you are not doing anything to control your weight. Your regular regiment includes healthy eating habits combined with physical activity, and your weight remains constant.

Genetically, the makeup of our bodies helps establish and link us to our individual set points. Thanks to our ancestors, our ideal weight, also known as the 'set point', is unique to each person. Body fat or weight that is maintained for an extended period of time (in terms of months and years) usually determines a person's weight 'set point'.

Muscle and fat make up over one-half of the body's weight; skin, bones, blood, and organs make up the rest. Men's bodies usually have a higher ratio of muscle to fat than women. The number of muscle and fat cells in the body determines individual variations in the amount of muscle and fat tissue in body weight. A person with a large number of muscle and fat cells will weigh more than someone with fewer muscle and fat cells.

The numbers of muscle cells in our bodies are predetermined before birth and remains throughout our lives (with a slight decrease in the golden years). We are all born with billions of fat cells. Some baby fat cells grow and mature considerably in the first year of life, and have been known to reach the size of adult fat cells. This is why it is crucial to keep active and in great physical shape as you mature in age.

The good news is that the size of cells change, and the size of those cells are partly within your control. Muscle cell size will be determined by use. Couch potatoes who choose to participate in very little, or no exercise – their cells shrink from atrophy (no use). Bodybuilders' cells often grow larger from hypertrophy (over-use). With moderate or occasional physical activity, such as aerobic exercise and recreational sports, muscle size usually remains the same.

Genetics and lifestyles have an impact on weight gain. Depending on these varying factors, the greatest change in fat cells will not be in size, but in number. Unfortunately, the number of fat cells increases, but they never decrease. The reasons for the constant increase in the number of fat cells are still in question. If you are genetically predisposed to have twice the number of fat cells than someone else, it can be expected that you will have a higher set point for body fat and body weight. Since we have the capability to grow more fat cells but not get rid of them, the only way to lose fat is by reducing the amount of fat in existing cells. Whether our fat cells increase, decrease, or remain constant in size can be largely affected by exercise, and the type and quantity of food we eat.

This is how it works: if a person eating a high fat diet changes his dietary habits to a low-fat, high complex carbohydrate regimen, the fat in each fat cell will be reduced even if the number of calories consumed remains the same, or is even modestly increased. If fat burning exercises are included in the program, this will further reduce the fat in each fat cell.

We should not feel as if we are prisoners of our inherited gene pool. Studies and research over the years have continued to encourage the containment of our fat cells during our growth years, which can be influenced by good exercise and nutritional dietary habits. As mothers, sisters, aunts, and grandmothers, we can see how important it is to encourage our children to be physically active, and to discourage them from a regular diet of junk foods loaded with fat and sugar. There are no guarantees what your set point will be, but you and your children will certainly be healthier because of your efforts. Here's the bottom line - in order to increase maximum caloric expenditure, you must burn off the calories consumed on a regular basis.

## METABOLISM AND WEIGHT LOSS

All of us have probably known someone who is extremely slender, eats large amounts of food, and never gains a pound. You probably also know people who insist that whatever foods they choose to eat automatically contributes to their weight gain. Again, genetics are a factor in how fast or how slow the body breaks down and dissipates the food consumed.

Hormones and metabolic rates helps explain the paradox that exists between those who nibble on different foods throughout the day and never gain weight, and the carbohydrate and calorie counters who believe they gain weight just smelling food being cooked. One client said she believed she could gain weight by inhaling the aroma of fresh baked donuts.

Most of us have very effective metabolisms. An efficient metabolism means you need less food to maintain your metabolism. So the more efficient your metabolism, the less food you need to consume. A fast metabolism will burn off weight, while a slow metabolism applies the food directly to your hips. The reasons our metabolism changes or slows as we age are due to the changes that occur in our body (body composition, muscle mass, and hormone levels decrease).

As we age, we continue to have less muscle mass and fewer calories are burned for energy needs, resulting in a slower metabolism. Keep in mind that food is still scarce in some parts of the world. Many people died of starvation back in the caveman days; there were very few, if any, fat cavemen or cavewomen. The main key to their survival was a slow metabolism that saved every calorie as fat, because it would be needed during times of famine.

The world revolved around agriculture, which was far less refined in those days. Any natural event - snow, drought, or flood could wipe out a year's crops and influence crops for years to come. Those humans with efficient, slow metabolisms survived. Those people who would be considered naturally thin in today's society died, because they did not have enough body fat.

Now, back to those folks who eat and eat and never gain weight. Their internal processes are so inefficient they need to take in as much food/fuel as possible just to keep their bodies going. There never seems to be enough left over to be stored as fat. Metabolically inefficient people are able to eat large quantities of food and never gain weight, or get fat.

If your metabolism is inefficient and slow, you are sluggish and tired all of the time. When you speed up your metabolism, you burn calories quicker, your energy levels are raised, and you feel great. Unfortunately, there is no perfect medication to make this happen. Medications that do exist have side effects; some will make your heart beat faster and/or your mind race. Both of these can put psychological and physiological stress on the body.

Maybe you are thinking you can do the job with exercise alone. After all, if you burn calories, you lose weight, right? Well, you will, but there are limits. Most people exercise one, or at most, two hours each day. Keep in that mind, a revved-up metabolism works 24/7. However, if you eat healthy foods and exercise regularly, the excess weight will come off, and consistently stay off.

Healthcare professionals have begun to encourage patients to set healthy weight goals, even if these weights are higher than what the body mass index charts recommend. This is particularly important for those people who have struggled for years to maintain or achieve a certain weight goal. For these people, achieving a low, or socially acceptable body weight is like fighting Mother Nature.

Finding your own healthy weight is not always an easy task, particularly if you have dieted on and off throughout your life (commonly known as yo-yo dieting). A reasonable, or healthy weight is the one you are comfortable with, is not too demanding to maintain, and poses no serious health problems.

**Here are some tips to help you find and maintain a healthy weight:**

- Look at your family background, as weight gain is genetic. If no one in your family has been, or is thin, chances are you will not be thin either. **GOOD NEWS!** You can lower your body weight to a healthy level.

- Take into consideration your bone structure and body shape. Someone with large bones will never be as thin as someone who is small boned and petite.

- Choose a realistic weight you feel most comfortable and happy with. This is important because body image and weight are often closely tied to our personal happiness!

- Think of your body as an engine and your metabolism as the rate at which the engine runs - step on the gas to raise your metabolism.

- Plan your meals and snacks ahead of time. Failing to plan sets you up for failure.

- Serve yourself small food portions.

- Eliminate distractions (TV, reading, or talking on the telephone) while you are dining.

- If you feel that you are out of control, keep a food diary to help you keep track of your daily food intake.

- Focus on eating more fruits, vegetables, grains, and high fiber foods to help you feel satisfied.

- Set a time to close the kitchen for the day after eating meals.

- Keep bottles of drinking water handy – your car, each room of your home. You will always drink more water if it is always around you.


## *NO MORE EXCUSES!*

Most of us can come up with plenty of excuses why we are not more active. We are either too young, too old, too busy, too tired, or think that we are already in good physical shape without exercising. These excuses may sound good, but they really are pretty flimsy....

**Here are a few excuses...I have heard over the years. I always have a solution for most of them.**

...I have no time

...I don't like to sweat

...I have a hernia

...It's boring

...I can't find anyone to workout with me

.... I don't like to mess up my hair

.... I just had my hair done

.... I exercised for a week straight...and I didn't lose a pound

People are always amazed, when I have a comeback answer for their excuse for not being more physically active. So...here it goes.

If you don't like to exercise because you have no time. Make some time; because when you get sick and the body shuts down, you have plenty of involuntary time on your hand. So keep moving to help boost and strengthen your immune system.

If you have hernia.... check with your doctor to give you suggestions about which exercises are safe for you try.

If you find exercising boring, maybe you have not found the right activity. Try to engage in physical activities that you really enjoy and try to do them more often.

Can't find anyone to workout with you? Oh well, you are on your own. Do it for yourself, and don't wait for anyone to get started on a physical fitness program.

For you ladies that hate to have your hairstyle out of sorts, or if you are afraid to mess up your hair-do. Try one of these options. Get a more manageable hairstyle, get a wig for back up, and finally there are just too many other hair options to name. If you have the will you will find a way!

For those ladies that do not like to sweat- Sweating is great for the body, because it helps to remove impurities from your pores. (That's why it is essential to drink plenty of water daily to help keep a good balance of water flow in the body. After all the body is made up of sixty percent water.

Remember: There are a variety of activities for the young, the old, and for those with little time to exercise. If you are already in good physical shape, you need to maintain some level of fitness activity if you want to remain in good shape. Remember, the body is a work in progress that requires constant attention to keep it going at peak performance.

***Food for thought: If you are really looking for an excuse not to exercise. How about making an excuse to exercise... Let's get moving!***

# PART II

## *FITNESS ESSENTIALS*

## *EXERCISE*

I think I have heard just about every excuse why people do not like to exercise, and the words 'painful' and 'tired' always comes up in the top three. Some of the excuses I have heard include, "I walk every day, all day on my job - that's enough exercise for one day" or "I get enough exercise getting in and out of my car" or "I am just too tired to exercise after a long day". The definition of the word exercise is NOT torture! Exercise can be described as any form of physical activity: taking the long way around your office when you are going to meetings, hand-delivering memos instead of sending them interoffice mail, chasing your toddler around all day, walking your pet, parking at the far end of the lot and walking the extra steps to your destination, or running a marathon. Some of us have been consistent in adhering to an exercise program for many years, yet others have good intentions when it comes to exercise, but either there is no time for exercise, or there is a loss of interest in an activity or piece of exercise equipment that sabotages a regular exercise regimen.

We are spending millions of dollars every year on exercise videotapes, treadmills, stair-climbers, workout clothing, exercise balls, and all of the latest books on the subjects of health and fitness. Yet, year after year we repeat the same pattern - we tell ourselves "That's it! I am going to start a fitness program, and stick with it this time!" We continue to rely on the newest fitness gimmicks that promise to suppress our appetite, trim off excess pounds, or create the impossible 'perfect body'. Some of these fitness techniques often guarantee unrealistic results in minimal amounts of time, while using minimal physical efforts.

It takes more than fitness gimmicks to get you on the right road to a fitness program. If you participate in an activity that does not measure up to your weight loss standards, there is a good chance that you are setting yourself up for disappointment and rapid exercise truancy. Find an activity to participate in that you find fun and enjoyable that also gives you the full benefit of looking and feeling great. After ten minutes of muscular movement, most people say they begin to feel better as they continue exercising. Scientists are still working on an explanation why exercise improves the state of mind. Whatever the reason, most people continue to attest to the 'feel good' feelings. Although you will have to commit to some form of physical movement, I am sure you would rather be happy and healthier, than sad or depressed, because it is truly the only way to live life to the fullest.

**Exercise is essential for good health and well being for many reasons:**

- Moving the body in the form of exercise assists in the prevention of the yo-yo dieting syndrome that forces the body into a state of deprivation.

- Natural appetite suppressant

- Regular exercise alters your body chemicals so you feel less hungry.

Exercising can be made fun. Once you begin an exercise program, make sure you start at your own pace, remain patient, and go slowly. As human beings, we often forget that it took years for our bodies to get out of shape, so it certainly will take time to get back on track. Be patient, and take your health and wellness progress one day at a time. Listen to your body to determine what level of fitness you can handle and start with a few minutes of exercise every day, then gradually, over several weeks, work up to a full 30-minute workout. You will be amazed how quickly the body responds to new physical activity. Pace yourself and be patient - as your body becomes accustomed to a regular routine of exercise, you will feel better, look better, and acclimate to your new positive lifestyle change.

Whether you are beginning a new exercise program, or if more than 10 percent of your body weight is beyond your ideal body-fat level, or you are 35 years or older, you need to start with a realistic fitness program. Your body needs gradual conditioning before you begin the kind of exercises best for weight loss and fitness programs. Don't set yourself up for failure. The body is not designed to keep up intense efforts over a long period. Pushed to the limit, the body soon runs out of stamina. If we pace ourselves, we can condition the body to get stronger, build endurance, and keep exercising at reduced levels for longer periods of time.

As we mature and our bodies age, our joints stiffen, and our bones become more brittle and more vulnerable to injury from physical stress. Age 40 is usually when most of us need to begin to take special care not to over-stress our bodies. If you are overweight, your joints and muscles are already bearing excess weight, and probably should not have additional stress. The extra weight is also contributing to your heart having to work harder. If you are obese or 35 years or older, you will need to participate in exercises that will give you a maximum workout with minimal risks. Walking, swimming, and stationary bike riding are excellent activities with the least jarring to the joints and skeletal muscles. It is always a good idea to consult with your physician if you meet any of the criteria above.

Okay, you still say you have no time to exercise. Remember, any physical movement is better than no movement. All you need to do is be consistent in your endeavors 3 to 5 days a week, and you will notice a difference in your energy and stamina levels, as well as look better. Start off gently, use the stairs instead of the elevator whenever possible, or park the car and walk the two or three blocks to the store. Skip the coffee and donut break and take a 15-minute walk. Shorten your lunch hour and walk for 10 minutes. Take your dog for a walk frequently. Whatever you decide to do, get moving! Use it - don't lose it!

## EXERCISE DEFINITIONS

The fitness industry offers many exercise options to help prevent boredom and exercise burnout. Some of the terminology used in the industry can be overwhelming to the beginner and even to the seasoned exerciser. Listed below are explanations to help clarify some of the terms and definitions of exercises and fitness equipment currently used by fitness instructors, health clubs, and personal fitness trainers. This crash course in terminology will help you gain a better understanding of exercise jargon, and help clarify any misgivings, or lack of understanding about your fitness options.

**Aerobic** - 'with air'. When the body exercises, it needs an extra supply of oxygen. Oxygen is the fuel the body needs, and the body delivers oxygen to the muscles continuously during aerobic workouts.

**Amino Acids** - two basic building blocks of the body that makes up proteins.

**Anaerobic** - 'without air'. Refers to high intensity activity, i.e., sprinting or heavy power weight lifting. The body, after a short duration of high intensity activity (less than 90 seconds) begins grasping for air, and usually a burning sensation occurs in the legs, forcing you to end the activity.

**Antioxidants** - vitamins A, C, and E, along with various minerals, that are essential for protecting our bodies from unstable cells, often called 'free radicals'.

**Assimilation** - the process in which foods are utilized and absorbed by the body.

**Atrophy** - 'withering away'. If you do not participate in some form of exercise as you age, your body will become weak, leaving the body with little to zero muscle mass to perform tasks that are necessary for day-to-day functions.

**Barbell** - a weighted bar that is used for weight lifting, usually 5 to 7 feet long, with a rigid handle and detachable discs (weights) at each end.

**Body Sculpting** - non-aerobic muscle toning exercises that help increase strength and muscle tone, while lowering the risk of bone loss. (A body sculpting class often uses exercise bands and free-weights to help to power up (makes the muscles work harder) on toning muscles.

**Burn** - 'going for the burn' (terminology used frequently) means working the muscles until the lactic acid in the body builds up, causing a burning sensation during endurance exercises.

**Cardiovascular Exercise** - body conditioning that strengthens the heart and blood vessels.

**Circuit Training** - moving at a rapid pace from one exercise apparatus to another while keeping the heart rate high (target heart rate). This form of training usually engages all the muscle groups while giving your heart and lungs a great cardiovascular workout.

**Dumbbell** - a short, weighted bar with a rigid handle and detachable discs (weights) at each end that is used for exercise.

**Frequency** - the number of times, or sessions a fitness activity is performed in terms of hours, days, or weeks.

**Heart Rate** - the number of times your heart beats per minute. (Your 'resting heart rate' is the number of beats per minute while your body remains at rest. Your resting heart rate should be between 60 and 90 beats per minute.)

**Kickboxing** - develops stamina and power along with building strength and muscle, improving coordination, balance, and agility. Choreographed Kickboxing to music uses a series of jump roping, air punching, and footwork normally seen in a boxing ring.

**Lats** - abbreviation for 'Latissimus Dorsi', the large muscles of the back that move the arms downward, backward, and in rotation.

**Lower Abs** - abdominal muscles below the navel.

**Pilates** - developed by Joseph Pilates, a carpenter and gymnast. These exercises are designed to work the large muscles of the body as well as the small ones. Over 75% of Pilates exercises are performed on an exercise mat, enhanced by using weighted balls, straps, poles, or bars. Pilates requires a great deal of concentration, control, and dedication. The program offers quality workouts for the complete body.

**Repetition** - or reps, is one complete motion of an exercise, or a combination of more than one complete motion. When you lift your arm and lower it back down, you have completed a repetition. The number of reps you do will depend on your fitness goals.

**Resistance Training** - defined as any combination of sets, repetitions, and every kind of training method from light to heavy systems. The secret of resistance training is to constantly challenge the muscles by increasing the resistance levels, repetitions, or sets. The results of a resistance program are determined by how often a person trains, the order, number of sets and reps, which translates into volume and intensity.

**Set** - a group of repetitions/movements. One set per muscle builds as much strength as doing three sets per muscle for the first few months of training. If you are a novice, or reacquainting your body to fitness, your initial goal should be to build strength and endurance.

**Strength Training** - a form of exercise using resistance while strengthening the muscular skeletal system. Increased bone density, ligament and tendon strength are some of the most positive results of strength training.

**Tai Chi** - a Chinese form of exercise that helps with stress management, and develops complete body awareness. This group of slow, flowing exercises can improve balance, flexibility, and strength. Advocates of Tai Chi give high marks to these movements for improved circulation, coordination, and balance while improving the muscular and nervous systems.

**Tubing** - known as rubberized resistance, tubing offers two options: tubing, and stretch bands. Handles can be attached to the tubing for durability and for adjusting the length. Tubing and stretch bands are lightweight, portable, takes up minimal space, and can be adjusted to different heights for creating exercises that are difficult to reproduce with free weights.

**Yoga** - a blend of movements offering strength, flexibility, and body awareness. The goal is to provide a union of the mind, body, and spirit. There are many forms of Yoga, some requiring less strength and flexibility than others. Explore your options to find a branch of this wonderful exercise that will offer your body and mind a perfect fit.

## TRACKING YOUR FITNESS PROGRESS

Okay, you've made it over one hurdle. You have altered your dietary habits for the better, decided on a fitness regiment you can stick with, and now you are on your way. How will you know if your fitness efforts are paying off? You are not quite sure how to track your progress, or know what fitness accessories are available. How much food do you eat to lose 1 to 2 pounds per week? How do you measure your body fat? What are muscle mass caliper measurements? What does circumference measurements mean in terms of weight loss?

As a Personal Fitness Trainer, the only time I evaluate a client's weight is during the initial fitness test assessments. I like to use a tape measure, calipers, or an electronic body fat analyzer for the client's initial assessment. I usually have the client weigh themselves first on their own scale, and than on my fitness scale. The client and I write down both weight readings and then tuck them away for safekeeping. For some people it is important to know how much they weigh at the onset of a fitness program, while others request that I write down both readings and file that information for another day. Whatever the case, I always ask the client to remove the scale from the premises or put it under the bed, behind the sofa, in the attic or in the garage. In other words, move the scale monster as far away as possible.

This may sound like a drastic measure, but not if you want to move forward and without sabotage in your muscle and endurance building endeavor. The only way to do this is to set up a fitness plan for success without distractions. If you are one of the people mentioned earlier and do not have a problem stepping on the scale on a regular basis, there may be a noticeable fluctuation in your weight, either up or down. There are many reasons for variations: water retention, female monthly cycle, thyroid problems, etc. After the first weigh-in with my client, I usually take circumference measurements every three weeks. This enables me to monitor the body fat and any physical changes in the body.

The bathroom scale has always been a tool for those losing weight to track their progress. Stepping on the bathroom scale to track weight loss progress works for some, while literally giving others a migraine headache. Here's a tip - stay off the bathroom scale until you feel you can work with the results, whether they are favorable or unfavorable. I personally do not recommend using the bathroom scale as a gauge for weight loss. I would rather you gauge your weight loss through the looseness of your clothing.

A successful weight loss program should consist of a well balanced diet, as well as a physical fitness program. In order to show progress on a fitness program, you need to eat smaller portions, and have frequent meals throughout the day for workout energy you can count on. There are no miracle diets to help you lose weight.

Many popular diets available today are low enough in calories to achieve weight loss, but can the favorable results be credited to lower calories and fewer carbohydrates? There is no magic pill to lose weight and successfully keep it off. Balancing and maintaining the diet is one of the most neglected rules for many dieters. Eating foods low in complex carbohydrates and consuming more protein seems to be the dietary choices for people who have tried every type of diet.

**To lose weight, you must consume fewer calories than you expend. Realize that it only takes an extra 10 calories a day to gain one pound a year. If you increase your energy expenditure, or decrease the number of calories consumed, you will gradually lose weight. Remember that a gradual weight loss of 1 to 2 pounds a week is considered relatively safe.**

To lose one pound per week, you need to determine your desired weight, and using the following formula, find the number of maximum calories you may consume in one day to lose one pound.

**Formula:** Your desired weight multiplied by 15 = _____, subtract 500 from that number = _____: this is your maximum daily calorie intake for losing one pound per week.

**Example**: a 190 lb. man wishing to weigh 180 pounds, multiples his desired weight by 15 (180 x15 = 2700 calories), then subtracts 500 (2700 – 500 = 2200 calories), calculates that the maximum number of calories he will be allowed per day in order for him to lose one pound per week is 2200.

**One pound represents 3500 calories; this number divided by seven (seven days in a week) equals 500 calories a day. When you use this formula, you will find the answer to your question on how many calories per day you should consume in order to lose 1 pound per week.**

The most rewarding part of any fitness and nutritional program is seeing results, and your weight loss progress can be tracked with the tools listed below:

**Muscle Mass Calipers.** The caliper measurements are based on the fact that one-half of the total fat content of the body is located in the fat directly beneath the skin. The most common areas for taking skin fold measurements are at the triceps, abdomen, and upper thigh. All measurements are taken on the right side of the body.

**Circumference Measurements.** A Gauge Tape Measure provides the tool to measure muscle gain, or fat loss. As you exercise and burn more fat, you will be getting leaner and stronger. Your clothes will usually fit looser, but the scales may not show your weight loss, since muscle is more dense than fat. Circumference measurements should be recorded every three weeks in the following areas: abdomen, buttocks, right thigh, right upper arm, right calf, and chest.


## *HOW LONG SHOULD YOU WORK OUT?*

How often, how long, and how hard you work out depends on what kind of exercise you decide to do and what you are trying to accomplish in your new workout environment.

Listed below are activities and the length of time each should be done that are necessary for the average healthy person to maintain a minimum level of fitness.(Included are some of the popular exercises for each category):

**Warm-up:** 5 to 10 minutes for exercises such as walking, slow jogging, knee lifts, arms circles, or trunk rotations.

*   Cardiorespiratory Endurance: 20-minute workouts at least 3 times a week of continuous aerobic rhythmic exercises. Aerobic exercises include brisk walking, jogging, swimming, cycling, rope jumping, rowing, cross-country skiing, racquetball, etc.

*   Flexibility: 10 to 12 minutes of daily stretching exercises performed slowly without abouncing motion. This can be included after a warm-up or cool-down.

*   Muscular Endurance: 30-minute workouts at least 3 times a week that includes exercises such as calisthenics, push-ups, and weight training for all major muscle groups.

- Muscular Strength: a minimum of three 20-minute sessions per week that include exercises for all four major muscle groups. Lifting weights is the most effective way to increase strength.

- Cool-down: a minimum of 5 to 10 minutes of slow walking, low level exercises, combined with stretching.

**Food for thought: Consider exercise a lifestyle endeavor for good health, instead of an instant weight loss program.**

## EXERCISING AND STAYING MOTIVATED

Okay, you have decided on a fitness program. You are on 'Motivation Mountain' and nothing is going to stop you now! Week one: your fitness workout at your health club is pretty productive, and you are on a roll. Week two: your muscles have stopped aching and you are starting to enjoy your workouts and feel good about your progress. Six weeks have now passed, and you are still going strong. You have not missed one of your workouts, you are still hyped about your new fitness and nutrition endeavors, your efforts are beginning to show and others are noticing your progress. So, it is really happening, you are really toning up your body!

So far, everyone you have met at your health club is upbeat, and the staff is helping you plan weekly workout schedules. How can you not succeed in your fitness goals? Now a few months have passed. You realize that one by one, your workout friends are dropping out. They either have scheduling conflicts and cannot continue on your regular workout days have lost interest, or something else more important than working out has become their priority. Six months later, you are still working out, trying to maintain a regular fitness schedule on your own. You have not seen any of your workout partners at the gym in months. Okay, this is about the time some people begin to experience a form of exercise burnout - learn to recognize the signs.

The first sign of exercise burnout begins when you start making excuses about shorter workouts, or skipping them all together. One of three things usually happens: you either stay focused on finding ways to jump-start your program, you go to the gym and socialize more than you workout, or you give up the program altogether. You tell yourself you will get back on the program after this weekend, or try a crash diet to look good for a special event. Days, weeks, and months pass.... now what? Start again. This time set a daily fitness goal and take it one day at a time. This helps eliminate the pressure we often put on ourselves when it comes to getting back on track with a fitness program.

I work with a variety of personalities on a daily basis to help them change unwanted fitness and dietary behavior. Some of these groups are special populations - children, seniors, plus-size women, prenatal women, worksite programs, etc. Over the years I have learned that all of these groups are much more responsive to a fitness and nutrition program if they are given the opportunity to determine their own fitness likes and dislikes; whether they like to exercise in the morning or in the evening, how many days a week they can dedicate to an exercise program, and where they will workout - at home, at a gym, indoors or outdoors. Once these decisions have been made, the individual's program will be more successful, as they commit to attaining their fitness goals.

The first step to ensure that your fitness program is a success for life is to consider all the physical activities you like to engage in. Most people desire to be active, but feel there is too much of a commitment to revamp their over-all lifestyle. Exercise should not be thought of as an imposition, but as an enhancement of the mind, body, and spirit to help you enjoy each day of your life.

**A fitness program should contain several components for variety:**

- **Flexibility Training** - this component will help one attain functional flexibility. Stretching should be an important part of the program, helping get the body on track to be functionally fit.

- **Muscular Strength and Endurance** - this involves exercising the skeletal muscles. A gradual increase in resistance is necessary for increasing muscle strength and endurance, eventually leading to gradual increases in intensity. The focus during workouts should be on the muscles, and allowing the body to adapt progressively to new challenges.

- **Cardiorespiratory Conditioning** - helps get the heart rate up to the target heart rate so the body begins to burn body fat. Frequency, intensity, and duration are important considerations. I recommend exercising 3 to 5 times a week at 50% to 85% of the target heat rate.

- **Cross Training** - offers many advantages, variety, and change to enhance workouts, prevent boredom, and help work off weight loss plateaus, while increasing fitness gains.

- **Muscular strength, cardio respiratory conditioning, and flexibility training** are primary factors of a well-rounded, balanced approach to fitness. Placing demand on, or overloading the muscles develops muscular fitness in the muscles in a manner in which they are not accustomed. When muscle overloading is applied progressively and sensibly, the neuromuscular system will positively adapt to demand.

To be successful in your new fitness and nutrition lifestyle, you must be convinced that your workout efforts will be effective. No matter how long it has been since you have been on a fat loss program, many people, just like yourself, have become leaner and fit by accepting the personal challenge of making a reasonable effort to stay on a lifetime program that leads to a healthy lifestyle.

How much time and effort will you need to commit to your fitness program? A few healthy changes to your current lifestyle - exercising a few minutes every day, and making moderate changes in your eating habits will result in tremendous benefits: a longer, more productive life, increased self-confidence, lower blood pressure, a sleeker, leaner body, more energy, improved appearance, greater resistance to stress, a stronger immune system, insomnia relief, and more. You can see that the benefits far outweigh the costs.

As we all know, life is a series of continuing changes, and people fear change. Yet, despite our current condition, the deep-rooted resistance to change often prevents some of us from making the physical and mental changes we know we must make in order to benefit from a health and wellness lifestyle.

Recognize that you, and you alone are responsible for the success of your program. I suggest that once you have decided to plan your fitness regiment, create a sense of urgency to do something about losing weight and getting fit. You may be familiar with the old saying 'pay now or pay later'. Case in point - the metabolic process that determines how much you eat is stored as fat becomes slower and less efficient with each passing day. The longer you wait to awaken the slumbering fat burning capabilities, the harder it is to increase the metabolic process (body fat burning).

### Try my 30-day challenge:

Every day for 30 days, drink plenty of water, (6 –8 glasses) exercise for 15 minutes, eat 3 to 5 small balanced meals, and take 10 minutes at the beginning and end of each day to meditate and reflect on your day. Think of at least one thing you have to be grateful for. Try to do a random act of kindness, every opportunity you get. (Pay for the next person's car wash, bridge toll, groceries at the store, gas at the gas pumps) I think you get the picture. Believe me if you are observant of others, the opportunity will present itself every day. After thirty days of these rituals you will find that you have created a hard to break HABIT. Try it. It works - it will change your life!

## STRETCHING

Health and fitness professionals as well as athletes have known the importance of stretching the muscles before and after fitness activities to avoid injury, and to enhance sports performance. Performed correctly, stretching also leads to an increase in the normal range of motion, leading to better flexibility. Flexibility can also vary between joints or the same joint on opposite sides of the body. This is a benefit to the athlete because the greater the range of joint movement a person has, the greater the amount of force that can be applied to the ground, water, or objects used during sports. Some folks do not understand how much the sedentary, or even the active person, can benefit from a few moments of daily stretching to increase flexibility.

Stretching also offers tension relief, helps with relaxation, and improving general health. The balance of flexibility and strength in all muscle groups enables the best possible posture to be maintained, and this is critical whether you are sitting, standing, driving, or performing an activity, in order to avoid strain and injury, in particular to the muscles and joints of the back. Stretching will not burn many calories, or help build your body like a professional bodybuilder, but a few minutes of daily stretching can be a wise body investment.

If you sit or stand for long periods of time, you are a prime candidate for implementing a stretching program. Many working folks tend to spend lots of time seated, driving cars or trucks, or slouching at keyboards and computer screens. Their muscles and joints are in abnormal positions for extended periods of time and this can habitually lengthen or shorten certain muscles.
These changes create a damaging domino effect that may lead to pressure being exerted upon other structures within the body, such as blood vessels, nerves, and organs.

Stretching helps maintain the strength and power of a muscle, helps prevent injury, and increases circulation to the area that is being stretched. Stretching is a vital aspect and basic element of every major type of physical activity. Start your stretch program with regularity. Try stretching at least 3 days a week, holding each stretching pose for 10 to 30 seconds, and then repeating the stretch 3 to 5 times.

Earlier I mentioned that stretching helps prevents injuries and increases circulation. Warming up the body before exercising is important, as this indicates to the rest of the body that it is getting ready for movement. I emphasize warm-ups and the importance of stretching the body because it mentally and physically prepares the body to be aware of the various parts and limbs of the body to be naturally placed during the stretching process.

When the body begins the stretching process, the increase in body temperature makes the muscles supple and flexible. Maintaining flexibility ensures that our joints and muscles can function at their optimal level throughout our lives. As you begin to stretch your muscles, concentrate on what you are feeling. Your body will let you know if you are stretching too quickly, pushing or pulling too much. When a muscle is stretched, messages are sent to the brain to tighten that muscle and stop the stretch. This reaction is known as a 'muscle reflex'. It is activated by the speed of the movement and helps protect the body from over-stretching, but it also maintains muscular control during normal body movements like sitting and standing.

Flexibility levels vary from person to person, depending on age, weight, and lifestyle. Flexibility or joint stiffness can be determined by three components: bone structure, connective tissues, and surrounding muscles. Following are some interesting facts about what happens to our bodies as we mature in age.

## *BODY CHANGES ~ 20's, 30's, 40's, 50's, AND BEYOND*

**20's** - Your bones reach their peak mass, and you can maximize bone density with weight bearing exercises. This will ensure stronger bones, helping to prevent osteoporosis later in life. At this point in your life, flexibility is not an issue at all, your body still burns calories at a good rate, and you are physically active-always on the move. At this age, you want to take advantage of your fast metabolism and try to reach your target weight before age 30. I remember being at this stage – if I wanted to drop a dress size in two weeks it was an easy thing to do. At this stage of my life, my sister girls who were more mature and had been **There** and **Done** that, were always telling me that I would see how difficult it would be to lose or maintain my current weight as I aged...Girl- were they right on the mark! Believe me when I say that now is the time to start a fitness program and you will never regret it neither will you body.

**30's** - The body's cardio respiratory system is slowing and is on the decline. Your metabolism changes and your body will burn calories at a slower rate. You begin to notice unwanted pounds (sometimes it seems like they appear overnight). You are probably wondering at this point of your life if it is possible to gain weight by inhaling the aroma of your favorite foods- because it seems to take twice as long to lose five to ten pounds. Your flexibility is decreasing. Since peak muscle mass has been reached, if you do not start to exercise now your body will begin to lose muscle mass and muscle elasticity. At this stage of your life you will began to lose six to twelve percent of lean muscle mass every decade. Without regular stretching and strength training exercises, your bones are more prone to injury.

**40's**- You may have wondered in your 30's about your weight loss endeavors- Now that you are at this stage of your life you have convinced yourself that your body is no longer burning calories at all! You may or may not be carrying extra weight at this junction. If so, the extra weight makes you feel slower, and you are likely to experience shortness of breath after performing simple activities such as walking up a flight of steps, unloading packages from your automobile, etc., as lung capacity declines without regular cardiovascular workout. The skin on the arms, legs and breasts begin to travel south. Fat cells are stored on the stomach, thighs, and buttocks. At this stage of your life you will need to start muscle-toning exercises. Loss of muscle mass causes you to lose speed and strength if you do not keep up with some form of flexibility activity. Gentle Yoga, Pilates, Tai Chi, and other relaxation techniques listed in this book will help work wonders for your body.

**50's and Beyond** - Your body is burning calories much slower than it did in your 40's, and you thought your consumed calories were not burning at all! You will need to eat less, or reconstruct your diet by using fat-free and low-fat food options to maintain your ideal body weight. Some folks at this stage feel weaker, and bone mass is lost rapidly, risking osteoporosis. Weight bearing exercises are essential to help strengthen your muscles, whether you use your own body for weight for resistance, or free weights. Keep your routine at a comfortable level. Try stretches for relaxation, brisk walking, and swimming.

Body massage also helps you rediscover your muscles, and works wonders for the body, soul, and mind.

You may be asking yourself, right about now-other then educational background- how does she know what happens in the 20's, 30's 40's and beyond. I have lived a few of the decades discussed and the ones that I yet have to experience- I see evidence of the effects of muscle deterioration on people in their advance years.

**THE GREAT NEWS** - It is never too late to start an exercise program. Start now, and get your body on the move by strengthening, building endurance, and participating in some form of cardiovascular activity on a regular basis. The physical and mental rewards will be everlasting

## *MUSCLE SORENESS*

Muscle soreness can happen to any of us at any time - beginning exercisers, home repair weekend warriors, even gardeners who work long periods of time pulling weeds, planting flowers, etc. This temporary pain is not partial - soreness happens to people who use the same muscles for extended periods of time, or who have worked the same set of muscles in new and different ways.

When you use muscles that have not been used for a while, or try a new exercise, or even a new training technique, delayed onset muscle soreness (DOMS) results from muscle overuse. This discomfort is caused by microscopic tears in the fibers of the connective tissue (the ligaments that connect bones to other bones), and the tendons that connect muscles to bones, or by muscle spasms and possible over-stretching. The degree of muscle soreness is usually related to both the intensity of the muscular contractions and the duration of the exercise.

During a workout, muscles lengthen and shorten, and the repeated contractions cause lactic and other acids, as well as proteins and hormones, to build up in the muscle tissue. Normally this can cause pain without injury, but if you experience sharp continuous pain, or a burning sensation, you should immediately stop the activity. (Note: lactic acid is gone from the muscle long before soreness occurs.)

After a workout it is important to provide ample time (at least 48 hrs), for the muscles to recover. This means that the strength workout frequency should be every second or third day. If you work out every day, do not work the same muscle groups; instead, work the opposing groups and secondary muscles. For example, work the chest and triceps one day, and biceps the next.

Here are some of the injuries that can occur as a result of not stretching, using correct exercise form, or cooling down after a workout:

**Ligament injuries** - occurs when momentum and jerking movements are used to complete the weight lift.

**Muscle soreness** - a good way to reduce sore muscles is to rest, drink lots of fluids (especially water), use ice packs on the sore area, and if possible, use periodic massage therapy.

**Sprains or muscle tears** - can be prevented if you warm-up, stretch, and cool-down properly.

**Tendonitis** - inflammation of the tendon can occur if the first set of exercises begins with lifting heavy weights and/or the muscles are not quite warmed up.

## MUSCULAR STRENGTH AND ENDURANCE

Muscular strength is the ability to exert maximum force, usually in one single repetition. Muscular endurance is the ability to repeat an activity many times, or hold a particular position for an extended amount of time. It is quite possible to train for one area or muscle group without the other, but training both areas will result in a more balanced performance in any activity you choose to participate in.

The benefits of improving muscular strength and endurance makes completing daily tasks easier, provides a reserve of energy, and increases the ability to complete more tasks. Workouts can help relieve stress and improve self-image through an improved physique. Self-esteem often improves when an individual begins to see gradual, positive changes to their body structure.

Building strong muscles will help our bodies stay lean and strong. The body that has more muscles will use up more calories even when just sitting around, the energy needs will increase, and the metabolism will speed up. Note: An average weight training session uses about 300 to 500 calories an hour. (Remember, it takes 3500 calories to gain one pound, and muscle weighs more than fat.)

Building muscles decreases the risk of developing health problems such as heart disease, diabetes, and cancer. Stronger muscles also improves problems in posture, a protruding abdomen, lower and upper back weakness, and protects the body from injury by cushioning falls better than fatty tissue. When these areas are strong, we stand taller, and walk with better balance. Strength training also helps slow down the aging process, as unused muscle shrinks about 10% with each passing decade.

Men and women pay for facelifts, have collagen injections, breast implants, and other cosmetic enhancements. There is no surgeon in the world that can inject the body with all-over naturally built muscles. Muscle is the least expensive beauty aid - all we have to do is use it! As we age, it is important to continue with some form of regular exercise so our muscles continue to get both stronger and more defined.

Muscle strength adds density to our bones and reduces the risk of osteoporosis. Our skeletal frame needs weight bearing exercise to encourage the production of more bone cells and calcium. Walking and running are great weight bearing exercises for the lower body and provides a great cardiovascular workout at the same time! Most of our bodies are already strong in this region of the body, so it is essential to give the body a well-rounded (upper and lower) strength-training program.

Scientific research has identified proven prescriptions for muscular strength. It is important to balance the fitness program with calisthenics, weights, variable resistance, and/or free weights. The objective is to place the muscle under tension for a sufficient time. Training should be specific; muscles should be trained in terms of angles, range of motion, and velocity of contractions. Repetitions, sets, and frequency play a major role in strength and endurance programs.

The difference between training for strength, and training for endurance is the level of tension in the muscle, the resistance used, and the number of repetitions. Using lighter weights does not provide enough stimulation for strength development, but if enough repetitions are performed, muscular endurance will develop progressively. . Although it is harder to go from 5 to 10 push-ups (because it takes strength), it is easier to improve from 20 to 40 chin-ups (this takes endurance). Remember, your genetic makeup and your dedication to fitness training determines your ultimate progress.

## WHERE TO BEGIN:

- For sedentary individuals and those individuals over 40, it is best to consult with your medical doctor before engaging in an exercise program.

- Dress comfortably - wear workout clothes such as sweat suits (cotton works best, because it allows your skin to breathe).

- Warm-up - I cannot emphasize enough how important it is to stretch before and immediately after physical fitness. Warming up cold muscles helps prevent injuries while giving your muscles the flexibility they need before engaging in an extended workout.

- Start by walking slowly, or try jogging for 5 to 10 minutes. Pause to do some light stretching. When you are stretching, make sure you stretch by using static stretch movements (stretching the muscles slowly and pausing for a moment).

- Cool-down - after a brisk walk or working out with weights, you need to cool down with slow, stretching movements (static movements) The post-stretch will speed up muscle recovery, and you will be ready to start your next workout a lot sooner.

- For the first few weeks, it is advisable for beginning exercisers to start their fitness programs with longer stretching movements and shorter workouts, until their bodies become acclimated to continuous and repetitive movements, and are ready for an extended workout session. You will be the first to know when your body is ready to progress to the next fitness level.

- Listen to your body. If you are participating in a physical fitness activity and cannot comfortably hold a conversation, give your body a break. Never exercise until your muscles are in agony- stop long before this happens. Again, more is not always better.

- Never work the same muscles on consecutive days.

- Immediate and advanced exercisers will want to burn at least 300 calories per exercise session.

Do not be surprised if in the beginning of your strength training program, you double, triple, or quadruple your muscle strength in just a few months. Because the body gets stronger in layers, some folks at the beginning of a strength-training program may experience skin tightening and muscle hardening under the skin. However, the body is resilient and will adapt to repetitions, sets, and frequency modes of exercise.


## CALORIE BURNING ACTIVITIES


Did you know... you need to burn 3500 more calories than you take in to lose one pound? To calculate the number for your exact weight, take the number listed next to the physical activity, divide by 100, then multiply by your own weight (in pounds).

Keep in mind that your body burns calories all day, even when you are not exercising. The number of calories you burn while resting will be lower than if you were participating in some form of physical activity. To keep your calories burning at a maximum rate all day, try simple things like parking a bit farther out in the parking lot and walking to your destination. Take the stairs; walk to the local market, park at one end of the mall and walk to the other end. These things can add up quickly. The end result is still the same - you must burn more calories than you consume to lose weight.

The information below gives you an idea of the calories used per hour in common activities. The list indicates how many calories your body will burn off during a 30 or 60-minute workout while engaging in some of the most popular physical indoor and outdoor fitness activities. The first set of numbers beside each activity reflects 30 minutes of participation, the second number reflects participating in the activity for 60 minutes. The numbers given are estimates only. Note: Calories burned vary in proportion to body weight, composition, and intensity level.

## ACTIVITY

Aerobics (high impact) - 320/660
Aerobics (low impact) - 270/540
Basketball (game-playing) - 159/550
Baseball/Softball - 159/317
Bicycling (6 mph) - 130/240
Bicycling (12mph) - 200/410
Bicycling (15 mph) - 320/600
Circuit Training (with weights) - 320/580
Dancing (swing) - 205/390
Dancing (line) - 138/258
Elliptical Trainer - 548/905
Football – 280/530
Golf (riding in cart) - 168/336
Golf (carrying clubs) - 170/340
Heavy cleaning, washing car, windows - 218/436
Hiking (incline) - 190/360
Hockey - 290/555
Horseback riding - 130/260
Ice-skating – 225/445
Kayaking – 150/300
Martial Arts/Karate - 150/300
Racquetball (casual) - 225/450
Rock climbing (ascending) - 388/722
Running (8 minute/mile) - 450/925
Running (10 minute/mile) - 360/730
Skate Boarding - 165/317
Ski Machine - 280/575
Soccer - 270/555
Snow shoeing - 290/535
Stair Step Machine - 310/618
Stretching/Hatha Yoga - 192/384
Surfing - 97/195
Swimming (freestyle) - 288/510
Tennis - 225/450
Volleyball (beach) - 90/190
Walking (flat terrain) (17 minute/mile) - 130/275
Water Polo – 280/480
Water skiing - 205/415
Weeding (garden) - 160/320
Weight Lifting - 270/510
Wrestling (5 minute match) - 180/387
Yoga – 120/240

## *REVIVE YOUR FITNESS WORKOUTS WITH CROSS TRAINING*

Most humans are creatures of habit, whether we perform the daily ritual of making coffee, eating fast foods, or using the same exercise program. Using the same fitness routine is a sure-fire way to experience boredom and delay 'desired' results. Cross training is fun and invigorating, and it increases the metabolism. The advantage of cross training is to work all the muscles in the body while performing a variety of fitness activities. My favorite cross training class includes a light warm-up while stretching muscles, calisthenics, Kickboxing, Pilates, and Yoga. The warm-up includes a stretch that gradually warms the muscles, preparing them for lots of movement.

Calisthenics helps to loosen tight muscles and creates more flexibility, muscle strength and endurance. Kickboxing gets the heart rate up to the target heart rate, and helps burn maximum calories. The gentle moves of Pilates helps create long, lean, toned muscles that improves the posture while creating core strength, and the mind and body connection involves elongating the extremities with slow, methodical, and precision movement. Lastly, the Yoga poses help the body relax, while helping create balance, serenity, and harmony.

Cross training is a popular method of exercise, incorporating a series of different fitness activities to maximize fitness workouts. If you are an athlete or fitness enthusiast, cross training gives you more training options in a single sport to achieve balance in your fitness program. The benefits of cross training allows you to exercise more muscle groups while providing relief to highly used muscles, therefore lowering the risk of exercise injuries. For example, if you run 3 to 5 times a week, you can alternate your running sessions with swimming. You will be giving your joints a rest while still participating in some form of activity.

Another benefit of cross training is conditioning different sets of specific muscles to help improve over-all muscle endurance. Remember, cross training works for everyone. Whatever your exercise of choice may be, cross training can help improve your muscle leanness, workout intensity, endurance, and increase your muscle strength. You can use a variety of physical activities every day, instead of devoting an entire workout to one type of exercise. Remember, the best way to avoid boredom and exercise plateaus is to change your fitness routine by using a variety of exercises, and changing the order of your workouts.

Cross training offers a wonderful way to remain active and fit, as you grow older. Take every opportunity to burn unwanted body fat. The more muscles you involve in your workouts, the better the chance to achieve all of your fitness goals. Cross training offers an additional bonus for your fitness regiment.

Athletes are well acquainted with the practice of incorporating a variety of exercises during a workout, and have used cross training for many years to prepare for competitions. The average person makes very little use of it, and most people have no idea just how well this training helps increase muscle mass. As we reach age fifty and beyond, it is harder to retain muscle mass because we exercise less and because it is harder to rebuild muscle. As the aging process continues, we may not be able to achieve the muscle mass we were able to retain in our youth, but with routine cross training, we can maintain our current muscle mass and strength.

If you plan to start cross training, start slowly as you would with any other fitness activity. The best way to begin a cross training program is to pair activities that will train different parts of the body on alternate days. Swimming with cycling, and rowing with running, are examples of cross training sports.

## CROSS TRAINING EXERCISE SUGGESTIONS

- Bicycling, rowing, cross-country skiing (20 minutes) and stretching (10 minutes)

- Jogging at interval pace (20 minutes) and stretching (10 minutes)

- Jogging at a steady pace (30 minutes) and stretching (10 minutes)

- Swimming (30 minutes) and Yoga (20 minutes)

- Walking (fast) with hand weights (30 minutes) stretching and upper body training (10 minutes), upper body weight training (30 minutes)

- Walking (fast-paced) (20 minutes) upper and lower body weight training or circuit training (30 minutes)

- Walking (normal pace) (30 to 35 minutes) and Yoga (20 to 30 minutes)

**Benefits of cross training exercise and specific sports:**

- Aerobic Dance - works major muscles, and provides an outstanding cardiovascular workout

- Cycling - great lower body conditioner

- Rowing - strengthens the whole body, particularly the thighs and upper back

- Skiing - (downhill and cross-country) excellent body conditioner.

- Cross-country burn more calories (no stopping and waiting at the bottom of the hill, or standing in line for a chairlift), and it also strengthens the shoulders and upper arms

- Stair Climbing - works quadriceps, and improves running performance

- Swimming - provides an aerobic workout as well as conditioning the upper body

- Tennis and Squash - cardiovascular conditioning

- Walking - increases caloric expenditure by walking vigorously while swinging the arms

**A few more words about Plateaus and Cross Training**

If you have been trying to lose weight and feel you are not seeing the results you desire, you may have come to a fitness plateau. Cross training will provide the change and the variation the body may need after an extended repetitive exercise program. When the body becomes acclimated to a regular fitness routine, it is not uncommon for weight loss and muscle gain to come to a standstill. Cross training introduces new elements to spice up the workout. When variations of exercises are introduced into a fitness regiment, the body begins to recognize the differences and responds by showing faster, and more satisfying results.

## *POWER WALKING*

Power walking is a natural activity you can do anytime and anywhere. This fast-paced movement of robust walking provides a challenging workout, boosts cardiovascular fitness, helps with weight loss, and helps you maintain your current weight while improving your posture. Power walking at the beginning of your day helps jump-start your metabolism to burn fat at a faster rate for the entire day, and the calories stored from the night before will be used up soon after you begin to exercise. Walking 30 minutes a day at least 3 times a week, and a balanced dietary plan is recommended for weight loss maintenance.

The whole body benefits from walking. Walking is a weight bearing activity, and helps strengthen bones while preventing diseases like osteoporosis. Power walking is a great alternative exercise and easier on the joints than high-impact sports. Walking on an incline also uses the larger leg muscles like the hamstrings and glutes, as well as the upper torso muscles. You will still enjoy some of the benefits of running and aerobics while increasing your heart rate. The vigorous movement helps you move faster, increasing your heart rate, thereby improving circulation, giving the body a full cardiovascular workout that will burn more calories. You can also train your body to stay upright in an aligned position while power walking, which will improve your long-term posture.

Here is my recommendation for power walking correctly: lean forward a bit from the waist, keeping the back straight to engage the abdominal muscles. Step smoothly from heel to toe. Use my analogy of an imaginary line; when walking along this imaginary line, it forces the body to rotate the pelvis while slightly extending the hips. The stomach is pulled towards the spine (navel to spine); the neck should be kept straight with the chin slightly down so the back remains straight. The arms should be held at 90-degree angles, and pumped gently back and forth with each step. As each step is taken, the heel is placed on the ground and the foot should roll forward, using the ball of the foot and the toes in one smooth motion, instead of 'pounding' each step. Walk with an open stride, look straight ahead, and keep moving.

The best way to learn to power walk is to practice walking fast in short stretches, with rest periods in between. Alternating intervals of high intensity walking with rest periods allows the heart, lungs, and muscles to work hard for short spurts, something they can do continuously. Try alternating 30 seconds of high intensity training with 30 seconds of recovery in between. Using this method, the body will acclimate itself and will eventually be able to maintain a high intensity pace for longer periods of time.

## WEIGHT TRAINING

Weight training can improve muscle strength, help tone and shape the body while improving performance in daily activities and sports. A weight training program offer many advantages; however, if you are not quite sure where, or how to begin a program, get professional training in proper lifting techniques to avoid potential injury.

I am often asked, " How much weight should a person lift when starting a strength training program?" A person should start by using as much weight they can lift correctly, and without discomfort, through a full range of motion for 8 to12 repetitions. When lifting weights, if your back is arched or the hips are thrust forward, you are probably lifting weights that are heavier than your strength capabilities.

If using free weights, make sure to start with a lightweight, and establish the correct technique before increasing the weight. As a rule, I always encourage women to use light weights (3-5 pounds) while performing repetitive moves. Over the years, I have encountered women who do not want to incorporate weight training into their fitness program for fear of bulking up their muscles. The truth of the matter is that using lighter weights (1 to 4 lbs.) correctly will prevent this. Doing 3 sets of repetitions (8 to 12) on workout days will help the body get stronger and leaner, while gaining a more sculpted look without bulking up.

The aim is to increase the weight to the next level once comfortable. As muscle strength improves, the amount of weight `lifted' should be increased in small increments. One can also 'overload' the muscles by increasing the weight. Resistance machines that work on selectively isolated muscle groups through their range of motion are usually easier, and safer for the beginner.

How often a person works out is as critical in building strength as the workout itself. Weight training should be done on an 'every-other-day' basis, because it takes 24 to 48 hours for the body to replenish its energy resources, while adapting to its improved level of fitness. Weight training every-other-day actually results in greater improvement than a daily workout routine.

Over-training and inadequate rest not only interferes with the results one is trying to accomplish, but may also cause injury. Ideally, training every-other-day is my recommendation for most people. Option: if you feel that starting with weights will be too hard for you, use your own body weight to perform the exercises. For example: doing bicep curls without weights.


## *FITNESS ON THE GO: RUBBERIZED TUBING*


If you are looking for a new way to enhance your exercise program, or searching for exercise equipment that requires little space, is lightweight and great for traveling, then stretch tubing may be a perfect match for you. This form of strength training emphasizes both eccentric and concentric contraction (lengthening and shortening) of your muscles, and the resistance is in both the beginning phase and the return phase of the exercise.

The secret of a successful resistance-training program is to constantly challenge the muscles by increasing either the resistance level, or the number of repetitions or sets that are performed. This is also known as progressive resistance, because one is demanding more work from the muscles and they are forced to adapt by getting stronger. As the tubing is stretched, the resistance gets greater. The resistance is greatest at the midpoint of an exercise when the tubing is at its most stretched point.

There are several varieties and levels of resistance tubing. Usually the thicker the tube, the greater the resistance will be. Each level of resistance is designated by a different color. The colors may vary from manufacturer to manufacturer, but as a general guideline, lighter (pastel) colors designate lighter resistance, and the darker colors, heavier resistance. There are various types of tubing, and it is always best to purchase tubing that is designed specifically for exercise. These usually have some type of handle or other accessory to help make workouts safer and easier.

There are two options for rubberized resistance: tubing and stretch bands. I like to work with tubing as it is better suited to exercise because of its durability, and the handles are usually pre-attached. Handles can be purchased separately for stretch bands, which also allows you to adjust the length. Both tubing and stretch bands wear down over time due to use, and exposure to heat and cold. One should always check for weak areas on the tube or band before each use, and replace them when necessary. All exercises can be done with either tubing or stretch bands, depending on preference.

Tubing is not designed for heavy strength training or bodybuilding, but more for body sculpting and defining muscles through high repetition exercises, or to complement an already existing weight training routine. As a Fitness Trainer, I find that my female clients prefer this form of exercise, because there is no chance of bulking up and building unwanted muscle. This method also works great for those who have sustained an injury; tubing allows one to exercise with light resistance to gradually increase the strength of the muscle. Physical Therapists and fitness professionals have used rubber tubing for rehabilitation and strength training for many years.

**Exercise with any form of tubing offers the great benefit of simplicity**; you need very few accessories to get a great workout. I do recommend adding a door attachment accessory, as it is quite simple to use. You can purchase a ready-made door attachment, or you can custom-make your own.

If you are going to make your own you will need rubber tubing, plastic handles, and a flat piece of nylon (6-12 inches long).

- First, decide what strength tube will work best for your body for strengthening and flexibility.

- Fold your tube in half, wrap and knot the nylon in the middle once or twice.

- Place the knotted part over the top or through the hinged side of a door. close the door with the knotted part protruding outward on the other side of the door, with both (handles) on your side of the door.

- Grab the handles and pull the rubberized tube straight towards you to make sure that it is secure.

- Test your door attachment for durability before beginning your exercises.

Advantages - lightweight and portable, takes up little space, resistance on both concentric and eccentric contractions, can be attached at different height levels to create exercises difficult to reproduce with free weights.

Disadvantage- resistance cannot be used for muscle building.

Note: There is no method for gauging the exact resistance level of an exercise. Therefore, trying to increase resistance in increments can be difficult.

**Here are a few tips to help get you started**:

- Always warm-up before starting your workout. Try to do a total body warm-up before you start tubing.

- Use proper posture. Maintaining proper posture greatly reduces the chance of injury and ma maximizes the benefits of exercise.

- Use proper form. Focus on the proper motion of the exercise, while concentrating on specific muscles that are being used.

- Breathe properly. Never hold your breath during any part of an exercise. Holding your breath can cause intra-thoracic pressure and raise your blood pressure, leading to dizziness, blackout, or worse. Inhale and exhale continuously throughout your entire workout.

- Stop if you feel pain. Stop exercising immediately, as continuing may cause, or Aggravate injury.

**A few words about...**

**Frequency-.** Exercise each muscle group 2 to 3 times per week. Allow a minimum of 48 Hours between exercise sessions for muscle recovery.

**Duration-** the duration of a weight training routine should take anywhere from 45 minutes
to one hour to complete.

**Fatigue-** Try to fatigue your muscles within the suggested within the suggested repetition range.

**Range of Motion-** Moving through a complete range of motion allows the muscles to stretch before each contraction, and increases the number of muscle fibers.

**Speed of Movement-** Exercise movements should be slow and controlled.

**Rest Intervals-** Allow a brief rest (30 to 60 seconds) between sets to give the muscles a chance to partially recover before working them again.

Changing your routine. If you want to make a change in your routine, wait until about the six-week point to do so.

Always, check with your physician before starting any new exercise program.

**Food for thought: Exercise, Try it, you just might like it!**

## *EXERCISING AT HOME: A HOME GYM*

I know how hard it is to make time to exercise. The fitness industry has tried every form of marketing to gain new members and retain its current memberships. Facility hours have been extended, free childcare is offered personal fitness trainers are readily at your service, and massage therapists are even available. Some of the more exclusive health clubs offer complete day spas, chiropractic services, snack bars, specialty classes, etc. If none of these options has worked for you, another option is to try working out at home.

If you want to get fit in the comfort of your own home, you need to decide where you want to set up your home gym, how much space you can dedicate to equipment, and if you need floor space for mat work. You need to cover all aspects of your personal fitness program: aerobic fitness, strength training, and flexibility. Your home does not need to be spacious, or stocked with the latest fitness technology equipment to become a functional home gym.

Starting up a home exercise gym is easier than you think. Your workout gym can consist of rubber tubing, a Yoga mat, workout videos, and a step. Or you can have a full gym set-up, with a treadmill, multi-gym work-out station, rowing machine, Pilates machines, a full set of free weights, Elliptical trainers (part stair-climber, part treadmill, part stationary cycle), and engage the services of a Certified Personal Fitness Trainer. Remember when setting up your home gym and purchasing fitness equipment to include an aerobic exercise plan (treadmill, Stairmaster, fitness videos, and other fitness equipment you can use for an indoor workout) for the adverse weather conditions during the year when you will be unable to do your workout outdoors.

Weather you decide to equip your home gym, on a minimal budget utilizing the existing space in your home, or renovate your home to build a custom home gym, you need to consider what your over-all fitness goals are, and what type of equipment you need to succeed in all fitness areas. However you decide to furnish your home gym, make sure it will be a functional fitness room that will help you attain your fitness goals.

It is essential, that you place the exercise equipment in an area or room that you feel most comfortable using. Make sure you have a plan in place so you are motivated to use the equipment (you may want to use an exercise tracking form or a journal for accountability). Use entertaining distractions such as a TV, stereo with upbeat music, and/or interesting magazines. Make sure the room has good ventilation and lighting. If you are serious about getting fit at home, treat yourself to a full-length mirror, as this will help keep you motivated to continue measurable fitness gains.

Before buying a major piece of fitness equipment, take measurements of the door opening as well as the area you intend to make into the designated fitness room. Shop around, because prices will vary. Fitness specialty stores are always your best bet because the equipment tends to be sturdier and more reliable. Most important, always take a test drive. Ask for a demonstration on every movable part, and make sure you clearly understand all of the exercise options available when using your equipment. If you have children, always check for safety features. This will help prevent accidents and injuries.

Remember to inquire about warranties and service plans. I always purchase an extended warranty; after all, the equipment will be used frequently.

Home gyms work well for people who have little workout time, are motivated to work out regularly on their own, and like the benefits of having the gym to themselves. This type of gym also works well for the individual who does not have time to work out at the gym on a regular basis, but keeps a gym membership because they like the social setting.

Before purchasing fitness equipment for a home gym, or committing your money and time for a gym Membership, you may want to consider a walking program or try fitness videos. This is especially true if have purchased exercise equipment before and used it for a coat rack, sold it (unopened) in a garage sale, used it for a ironing board, or walked by it on a daily basis promising that tomorrow would be the day you start your fitness program, but never got around to it!

# PART III

## *THE MIND AND BODY FITNESS CONNECTION*

✳*

## *BREATHING*

Breathing. Why would anyone write about breathing? After all, it is something that we do all day, every day. Let's all take a deep breath. How long has it been since you allowed yourself to slow down and take a long deep breath for relaxation? There is a difference between sighing heavily, and taking the time to breathe deeply in order to get oxygen deep down into the diaphragm. We are all in such a hurry, running from point A to point B, that most of us do not realize that we are just not taking time to stop and smell the flowers, or watch the birds flying in formation above our heads.

I remember a few years ago when my husband asked me why was I always making the sound of an over-exaggerated sigh, and I would always ask him what he meant. One day I was working alone in my office and let out a loud sigh - then I understood what he was talking about. From that day on I realized that not only was I sighing throughout the day, but those folks I came into contact with were doing the same thing. Even though we were making the same sounds of desperation in our breathing, I don't think anyone was aware that they were doing it, and or how frequently the sighs came and went.

Unfortunately, most people function on a daily basis by breathing incorrectly. Some folks do not realize they are not using their lung capacity properly to perform the job it was designed to do. Breathing to the point of experiencing a full breath usually takes awareness and practice. Once you have mastered the art of taking in a full breath, you will not only understand what it means to utilize the lungs to their full capacity, but experience how a complete breath really feels.

**Breathing properly can help reduce stress.**

**Try this mini-breathing exercise for stress reduction:**

- Find a quiet spot and sit, or lie down

- Place your hands on your stomach on each side of your navel

- Inhale slowly and say to yourself, "I am..."

- Exhale slowly and say to yourself, "...very relaxed."

- Let your arms drop down to your sides. Continue this process for 3 to 5 minutes

**Repeat this exercise throughout your day and whenever you feel the need to relieve stress.**

**Try this exercise if you need to relieve stress, relax or meditate. This exercise can be practiced seated or standing.**

**Practiced seated or standing:**

Inhale slowly as you raise your shoulders towards your ears
Exhale slowly as you lower your shoulders back to their original position
Inhale as you slowly expand your chest
Exhale as you slowly relax the entire body
Inhale slowly as you expand the abdomen
Exhale slowly as you release the air from your lungs

Breathing is totally involuntary. You cannot inhale and hold your breath for long periods of time - if you do, you will black out. As soon as you black out, your body begins to breathe again.

**Controlled** breathing is often referred to as breath control breathing. This form of breathing relies on intentional control of our breathing for beneficial results. The results differ from altering the breath, or the period of time of the inhalation and exhalation. As the popularity of Yoga continues to grow, breath control exercises will be practiced for years to come. This form of breathing is often used as fast belly breathing, alternate nostril breathing, and intentional hyperventilation. If you are interested in exploring more options on this form of breathing, you can find the information in various Yoga books.

**Conscious breathing**, also known as breath awareness, is practiced in many spiritual traditions such as Buddhism, Hinduism, Taoism, Islam, and Christianity. This form of breathing is also used in meditation practices as well as awakening and self-development.

**Focused breathing** is directing the breath to a targeted area in the body. This form of breathing is often used for self-healing, and coupled with movement, can be used to direct the energy of our breath to our skin, muscles, organs, bones, etc. This form of breathing, also called 'breathing through visualization', helps focus on breathing into a specific place of the body. Focused breathing is used in the mind and body exercises of Pilates. Before you engage your body in the mind and body movements of Pilates, you are encouraged to visualize the movement of the extremity you are about to exercise, while concentrating and coordinating the breath with the movement.

When you work your breath and body in unison, you will find that you can breathe easier and deeper. You will notice that you are able to reduce stress, help strengthen the immune system, and increase your quality of life. When you breathe this way, you may begin to notice that you are rushing around less, find that you are able to deal with stressful situations a bit easier, and are getting more gains from your exercise program.

**Let's take a moment to observe your body positioning:**

• Is your head balanced freely on the top of your spine?

- Are your shoulders braced up toward your ears or slumped forward?

- Are your stomach muscles relaxed?

- Do you have bad posture?

Did you know that years of bad posture could affect your breathing and create changes in your body that may restrict your natural movement? When you have bad posture, your lungs are not able to expand to their fullest capacity, resulting in what I call thoracic, or rib breathing (the inhalation and exhalation is constricted to the chest area). This kind of breathing many people accept as normal, but it is not. Relax, all is not lost, there is no right or wrong way to breathe, you just need to break the cycle of a lifetime of learned bad habits of poor posture while walking, standing, and sitting.

**Interesting facts about breathing-**

**Did you know...**

...The average person reaches peak respiratory function and lung capacity in their mid 20's? Then they begin to lose between 9% to 25% of their respiratory capacity for every decade of life! Unless you are already doing some type of fitness, your breathing capacity will decline as you age. As your breathing capacity declines, your general health will suffer, possibly shortening your life. So...if you haven't already started, what are you waiting for? Get moving. You will feel better in mind, body, and spirit.

...Most people have unhealthy breathing habits? Many of the clients I have worked with over the years have had to learn to breathe correctly before I could even begin to set up a customized fitness program for them. I have noticed that most people hold their breath, or breathe high in the chest (topically), or worse yet, in a shallow, irregular manner. What is really interesting is that most people do not realize their breathing patterns have become an unconscious bad habit, accidentally formed over the years.

... Incorrect breathing patterns can actually trigger stress and anxiety reactions?

... Heart attacks, cancer, strokes, pneumonia, asthma, speech problems, and almost every disease known to humans can be worsened, or improved, through the quality of our respiration through breathing?

...The respiratory system should be responsible for eliminating 70% of your metabolic waste? The remainder should be eliminated thru defecation (3%), urination (8%), and perspiration (19%). So, if you think that going to the bathroom, or frequently working up a good sweat is important, then just think how important it is for you to use optimal breathing!

## MIND AND BODY FITNESS

In the past, the fitness industry has largely neglected the mind and body integration. At the beginning of the 20th century, the very idea of coordinating, or balancing body and mind was little appreciated by most physical gurus. By the end of that century, the concept of introducing 'spirit' into the exercise equation still stretched the limits of appreciation of many fitness trainers, instructors, and students.

In recent years, there has been a renewed interest in mind and body integration. The appeal and attraction of mind and body exercise have become popular with fitness coaches and athletes who participate in sports like football, basketball, soccer, and other sports that require core strength. Seniors are learning how to gain more strength and develop flexibility. Baby Boomers are renewing their fitness vows and realizing they do not have to do high impact aerobics to lose inches. Lastly, younger generations are learning how to challenge their bodies in a safe and effective way. No matter what fitness level a person has attained, these diverse groups all have one thing in common - they have begun to realize the full benefits of mind-body concepts. The focus of the mind-body connection is the result, instead of the process, because the exercise being performed is the process.

In the 1970's, the high impact 'go for the burn', 'no pain - no gain' mentality ruled. In the 80's, step aerobics were the popular fitness trend, and in the 90's, resist-a-ball, tubing, body pump, and free weights were the rage. Currently, running long distance miles, bench-pressing heavy weight, and core strength training has become the trend.

The mind and body fitness connection is not a new concept for the fitness industry, but the strategies differ from the traditional concepts of physical fitness. The terms 'mind and body fitness' are rapidly changing as a variety of new fitness programs awaken and energizes the spirit, as well as the mind and body. Therefore, I have decided to put more emphasis on the mind and body exercises of Pilates and Yoga, because they are two of the most popular forms of mind and body exercises used today in Western and Eastern cultures.

Your mind and your muscles must be in unison with the body to gain 'inward focus'. This is achieved by being aware of what you are feeling in your muscles as well as being aware of your breathing. Emphasis is placed on the present, not the future; therefore, there is no goal but a continuing practice, which can lead to a lifetime of well-being.

## PILATES

Pilates (pronounced pil-lat-eez) was named after Joseph Pilates, a former carpenter and dancer. Pilates was frail and sickly, and suffered with rickets as a child. The Pilates method originated from his determination to strengthen his body. Pilates is said to be one of the most powerful mind and body exercises because it engages the mind while improving the body; concentration, and attention are called upon every movement. The powerful movements of Pilates develops all at one time what most exercisers need - strength, flexibility, muscle endurance, coordination, balance, and good posture with minimal or no risk of injury. The Pilates method has more than nine decades behind its tried and true formula for successful results.

The mind-body conditioning method combines both Eastern and Western philosophies of physical and mental development, and aims to promote neuromuscular harmony, balance, and coordination, while increasing strength and flexibility. The Pilates method at the time was called muscle control, or 'The Art of Contrology'. The original sets of 34 exercises were performed individually, on a mat, without aid or assistance from any machinery or equipment. Some of the movements have been expanded, and sometimes modified by trainers and certification organizations around the world to add more variety to the mind and body exercises. However, the focus on strengthening and stretching the body is still an essential ingredient of all training.

Pilates is a method of conditioning the body by stretching, while creating a streamlined shape. The movements are designed to work with the body, not against it. Pilates emphasizes ease of motion and economy of muscle use. Several of the movements are inspired by Yoga, and are patterned after movements of zoo animals such as swans, seals, and large cats.

Moving smarter, not harder, is what appeals too new and beginner Pilates participants. The slow, methodical movements are being recommended more and more by doctors for patients who suffer from back ailments and poor posture. (The most important muscle groups in the abdomen, back, and trunk are often called the 'core', 'center', or the 'powerhouse', because these are the muscle groups responsible for stabilizing our posture while protecting our organs, and maintaining over-all stability through flexibility and tone.) Pilates movements are proving to be very beneficial in strengthening muscle groups. My fitness colleagues are adding more and more of the mind and body movements to their customized programs, getting great physical results in shorter periods of time.

Although there are no miracle antidotes or guaranteed fitness results, Pilates has been classified as the next best thing to a cure for attaining a perfect body. Through consistent and faithful practice you can expect beneficial outcomes such as gaining strength, vigor, control, intensity, and more energy. Often called one of the safest workout techniques, no other exercise system is so gentle to your body while giving it a gradual, challenging workout. Many of the exercises are performed in reclining or sitting positions, and most of the exercises are low impact with some weight.

To add variety to my Pilates classes, I teach a class that integrates Standing Pilates, cross training, and core training all in one session. My classes are user friendly for all fitness levels since I teach modified, intermediate, and advanced movements in one class. In an ideal Pilates session, most instructors prefer that the class start and work at the same level for six weeks, and then graduate to the next level. Since most of us have other obligations (called life), I do the next best thing and teach three classes in one, emphasizing body awareness, non-competitiveness, and working at your own individual pace. It is truly amazing and rewarding to watch the progress of each participant during every session.

Regular practitioners all agree that in ten pilates sessions you will feel the difference, in twenty sessions you will see the difference, and in thirty sessions, you will have attained a whole new body. If you are young or old, athletic, a fitness backslider, a couch potato, or somewhere in between, once learned, the essential elements of Pilates can work for you indefinitely. Pilates' popularity continues to grow, because it offers body movements for the sedentary, the disabled, and yet is still challenging enough for the strongest fitness buff.

In a few weeks, you can expect to see and feel many changes in your new Pilates body. Your abdominal wall will feel firmer, your legs will begin to attain a toned appearance, you will stand taller, and your movements will become lighter and effortless when you walk. Your posture and breathing will improve, you will develop longer and leaner muscles, increased bone density, greater flexibility in your spine, and improved self-esteem. Now that is a list of successes!

Since Pilates conditions and sculpts the body, don't be surprised if your friends begin to tell you how great you look, or ask if you changed your make-up or did something different to your hair. You may or may not have made make-up or hair changes, but the changes you have made are subtle: you have reconditioned and sculpted your body. Sure, you may have lost a few pounds, but the number of inches lost may be greater than lost weight. What your friends are seeing is the new and improved you. You are probably standing taller, have more energy, and are more flexible, therefore look and move differently. Most of your friends will first ask if you have changed something about yourself, and then ask if you have lost weight.

Although Pilates is a great core conditioning exercise - it is not a cardiovascular exercise. Pilates sessions should be used to enhance your fitness program, as it improves muscular endurance and flexibility. I recommend participation in some form of cardio exercise 3 to 5 times a week. Cardio-Pilates or Power Pilates (core movements implemented at a faster pace, often using light weights and resistance bands) is slowly becoming more popular, because it offers a combination of fast-paced vertical movements, as well as a matwork program.

Whatever your preference, you are sure to find a class that suits your individual needs. As you begin to grasp the concept of this unique mind and body exercise, you will find that you are most likely to sweat as you segue from one Pilates movement to the next. Your core (abdominals and lower back) will get stronger and your muscles will began to lengthen over a period of time.

The great news about Pilates is that you won't get bored. For every move you think you have mastered, Pilates has a move with another version, or one that is different and a little bit harder. Anyone can benefit from Pilates; no matter how long you have been a student, how strong you have become, or how much endurance you feel you have gained, Pilates can still be found to be very challenging.

## PILATES PRINCIPLES

"Physical fitness is the first prerequisite of happiness. Our interpretation of physical fitness is the attainment and maintenance of a uniformly developed body with a sound mind, fully capable of naturally, easily and satisfactorily performing our many and varied daily tasks with spontaneous zest and pleasure" - Joseph Pilates

The Pilates Principles are whole body health, whole body commitment, and breath. Properly performed, Pilates becomes the vehicle for the body to reach its full potential.

Execution of the Pilates exercises require:

- Balanced muscle development

- Breathing

- Centering

- Concentration

- Control

- Precision

- Rhythm

Some of the many benefits from following the Pilates Principles:

- Coordination

- Efficient Movement

- Flowing movement

- Improved posture

- Mobility

- Rejuvenation

- Self-awareness

- Strength

You are on your way to creating a healthier mind, body, and spirit!

Before we get started with the mind and body connection movement, let's discuss the basics.

## PILATES GENERAL GUIDELINES

Perform exercises on a cushioned, non-stick mat with shoes off.

Keep movements controlled and fluid, not jerky or stiff.

Avoid locking elbows or knees when straightening arms or legs.

Keep lower back imprinted (pressed flat) when lying on your back with legs in the air.

Keep pelvis and shoulders in place during movement of arms and legs.

Keep abdomen flat (navel to spine).

Exhale when bending torso, and inhale when straightening torso.

Inhale through the nose and exhale through the mouth, emphasizing the exhalation.

Using the diaphragm, inhale, pulling the breath inward so your rib cage rises and your obliques (sides) elongate. Exhale by emphasizing the exhalation.

Avoid tilting the head forward; place the chin to chest, when rounding spine.

# BODY AWARENESS WARM-UPS

The purpose of the body warm-up exercises is to help you become aware of the shape of your body, breathing, movement, and most important —you will learn how to recognize, support and transfer your body weight, while your extremities are in motion. Through patience and persistence you will successfully accomplish mind and body integration by following a few guidelines:

- *Find a quiet and serene area where you will not be disturbed.*

- *Stand in place and practice your breathing through your diaphragm.*

- *Inhale through your nose, exhale through your mouth.*

- *Extend extremities without locking them.*

- *Relax and feel your mind and body unite.*

# BODY AWARENESS WARM-UPS

**1** | Stand with your feet in a tripod position (heels together, feet pointed outward). Inhale as you raise your arms over your head.

**2** | Exhale. Bend forward, placing your hands on your shins.

**3** | Inhale. Slowly roll your body up to a standing position.

# BODY AWARENESS WARM-UPS

**4** Inhale. Raise your right arm over your head, and exhale as you lower your right arm.

Exhale. Raise your left arm over your head, exhale as you lower your left arm.

**5** Inhale. Raise both arms, extend arms to shoulder height.

**6** Exhale. Bend forward, extend your arms towards your toes.

# BODY AWARENESS WARM-UPS

**7** | Inhale. Slowly roll your body up to a standing position, then exhale.

**8** | Inhale. Place your hands on your hips.

Exhale. Place your chin to your chest.

# BODY AWARENESS WARM-UPS

**9** | Inhale. Slowly raise your head, continue the movement towards your shoulder blades.

Exhale as you lower your head back chin to chest.

**10** | Inhale. Place your right hand on your hip.

Exhale. Lean your head to the right side (right ear towards your right shoulder). Inhale. Place your left hand over your head towards your right ear.

Exhale. Gently move your head towards your left shoulder. Inhale.

Repeat on the left side of the body.

# POWER PILATES PLUS

## A Few Words About...The Pilates Principles

*The Pilates Principles involve total mind and body commitment - **Breathing, Concentration, Control, Centering, Precision, Isolation** and **Movement** while engaging the mind and body as one unit.*

*Execution of the Pilates exercises requires:* Relearning basic functional principles and guidelines.

*Proper Breathing -* You will need to change your breathing habits - Pilates breathing is often called lateral or diaphragmatic breathing, because the abdominal muscles are contracted in order to strengthen them. As you inhale through your nose, exhale through your mouth (imagine that your navel is being held inward towards your spine by an invisible band), inhale from the chest area, (while you are still holding your navel inward toward your spine).

*Concentration -* The benefits of concentrating are worth learning. You will gain better mental clarity and reduce stress, while increasing your ability to focus and visualize your next movement.

*Control -* You will need to be in control of all your movements - imagine that

you are working against an imaginary resistance force as you systemically perform the moves.

*Centering -* The body should always work in unison; all of the movements are stemmed from the center of the body - the abdominal muscles, also called the core.

*Precision -* Movements should be implemented with grace and precision as you move your extremities in space.

*Isolation -* Through muscle isolation, Pilates helps to identify weak muscles and strengthen those areas of the body through muscle balancing.

*Movement -* The slow, continuous and controlled movements should stem from your most stabilized muscles (shoulders to hips). Joseph Pilates often called this part of the body the "powerhouse" or control center.

# POWER PILATES PLUS

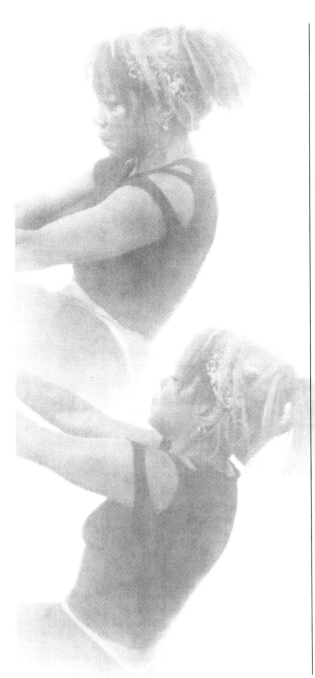

## Pilates General Guidelines

• *Start your Pilates practice in a quiet room where you will not have distractions. Use this time to replenish, center, and create balance and serenity.*

• *Perform exercises on a cushioned, non-stick mat with your shoes off.*

• *Keep movements continuous, controlled, and fluid, not jerky or stiff.*

• *Avoid locking elbows or knees when straightening arms or legs.*

• *Keep lower back imprinted to your mat (pressed flat) when lying on your back.*

• *Keep pelvis and shoulders in place during movement of arms and legs.*

• *Keep abdominal muscles flat (navel to spine).*

• *Inhale to prepare for movement, exhale when you execute the movement.*

• *Inhale through the nose and exhale through the mouth.*

• *Avoid tilting head forward; chin to chest, when rounding spine.*

• *Be patient. Pace yourself - and ease into the movements.*

*NOTE: Some of the Pilates moves have been shown with modifications, others do not offer a suitable modification. Proceed with caution.*

# POWER PILATES PLUS EXERCISES

## Hundreds:

***Emphasis*** - *This core exercise will get your blood circulating, while strengthening your abdominal muscles as well as your arms and shoulders.*

**A** Lie on your back with your arms to your sides - imprint your spine onto your mat. Lift your legs and bend your knees to your chest at a 90-degree angle. Inhale to prepare for the move, exhale to execute the move.

Raise your head and look at your navel.

**B** Pump your arms up and down in unison with 4 short inhalations, repeat with 4 exhalations.

Repeat this exercise 10 times or 100 breaths.

### Challenge:
Extend the legs at a 45-degree angle.

# POWER PILATES PLUS EXERCISES

## Single Leg Circles:

***Emphasis -*** *Strengthens and stretches the leg at the hip flexor.*

**A** Lie on your back with your arms to your sides - imprint your spine onto your mat.

Extend one leg towards the ceiling at a 90-degree angle.

**B** Inhale as you make a half circle, exhale as you complete the circle. Repeat.

Slowly rotate the leg in a circular motion (about hip width).

Repeat this exercise 6 times clockwise, 6 times counter clockwise.

### Challenge:
Continue anchoring one leg, while performing the circular rotation at a 45-degree angle.

### Modification:
Slightly bend the opposite knee when performing the circular movement.

# POWER PILATES PLUS EXERCISES

## Single Straight Leg Stretch:

*Emphasis - Stretches the hamstrings and lower back while working the core.*

**A** | Inhale. Bend both knees to a 90-degree angle.

**B** | Exhale. Extend your right leg at a 90-degree angle, (extend left leg about 6 inches off the mat.)

Inhale and switch legs quickly, and place hands on the left ankle).

Exhale. Pull the left leg towards your forehead - (pulsating) twice, inhale as you switch.

Inhale and exhale while switching legs like scissors.

Repeat exercise 6 times (6 times on each leg).

### Modification:
Place your hand on your knee, if you cannot reach your ankle, move legs between a 45- and 90-degree angle, while switching legs.

# POWER PILATES PLUS EXERCISES

## Double Leg Stretch:

***Emphasis*** - *Stretches the legs and arms, while stabilizing the Powerhouse.*

**A** Lie on your back, bring your knees into your chest while holding your ankles.

**B** Inhale, extend your arms and legs to a 45-degree angle.

Exhale as you stretch your arms out to your sides.

Inhale, reach for your ankles, exhale as you bring your knees into your chest.

Repeat exercise 6 times.

### Modification:
Extend your arms and legs to a 90-degree angle.

# POWER PILATES PLUS EXERCISES

## Rocker with Open Legs:

*Emphasis - Improves balance, stretches the hamstrings, strengthens the lower back, stimulates the spine.*

**A** | Balance on your tail bone - sit towards the front of your mat. Sit with your legs in front - knees slightly bent.

Inhale. Extend your right leg, (grab ankle) and left leg (grab ankle) between a 45 and 90-degree angle (in the shape of a V), then exhale.

**B** | Inhale. Extend both legs, while keeping your balance, (pulling in your abdomen).

Then roll backwards on the mat until the shoulders touch.

**C** | Exhale, roll back up and balance on your tailbone.

Repeat exercise 6 times.

### Challenge:
Extend both legs at the same time into the V position.

# POWER PILATES PLUS EXERCISES

**A** Sit on the mat with your legs and arms extended as far as you can - point your toes, and pull your navel to your spine.

Sit as tall as possible.

## The Saw:

**Emphasis** - *Stretches the hamstrings. Improves mobility. Helps to squeeze toxins from the body. Stretches the upper back, works the waistline.*

**B** Inhale. Twist to the right as far as possible, exhale, bend forward and downward.

Extend your left arm past your right foot, simulating the of a sawing motion. The right arm is stretched behind your back as you stretch forward.

Repeat the movement on the opposite side of the body.

**C** Complete the movement by going back to the starting position.

Repeat exercise 6 times.

**Modification:**
Sit tall, extend arms and legs only - twist slowly, from side to side (do not lean forward).

# POWER PILATES PLUS EXERCISES

## Spine Stretch:

*Emphasis - Stretches the back, hamstrings and hip flexors.*

**A** Sit tall, with your legs in front, knees are slightly bent.

Inhale. Lean forward - as if you were rolling a ball up over your stomach, (toes pointed).

Exhale as you extend and stretch your arms (shoulders relaxed).

**B** Inhale. Start to roll your back up by using your core (abdominal) while continuing to extend your fingers forward as you sit back in the starting position.

Repeat exercises 6 times.

### Challenge:
Extend your legs - flex your feet, lean forward, touch your toes and rest your head on the mat.

# POWER PILATES PLUS EXERCISES

## The Criss Cross:

***Emphasis*** - *Strengthens your back, trims your waist area, while working your obliques (love handles).*

**A** Lie on your back, place your hands behind your head, lift your upper body until your shoulders are raised off of the mat.

Inhale, bend your right knee to your chest, and bring your left elbow towards the right knee, while extending the left leg at a 45-degree angle.

**B** Exhale, bend your left knee towards your chest and bring your elbow towards the left knee, while extending the right leg at a 45-degree angle.

Repeat exercise 6 times.

**Modification:**
Extend legs at a 90-degree angle.

# POWER PILATES PLUS EXERCISES

## The Neck Pull:

*Emphasis - Improves posture, strengthens the powerhouse, stretches the hamstrings.*

**A** Lie on your back, (feet flexed) hands placed behind your back.

Inhale as you place your chin to your chest.

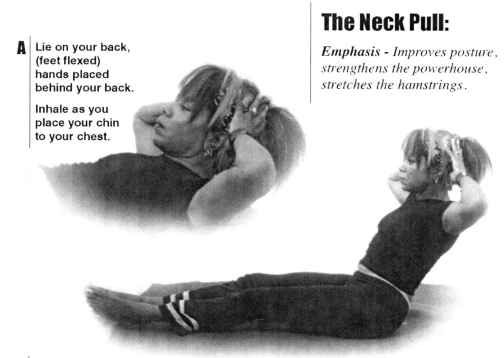

**B** Exhale. Round your back over your thigh, (navel to spine). Touch your forehead to your knees, elbows remain at your sides.

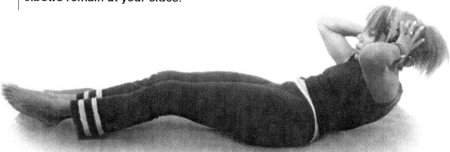

**C** Inhale. Round your back, exhale as you recline back imprinting your back on the mat.

Repeat this exercise 6 times.

### Modification:
If you are unable to roll up to a seated position, simulate the position by scooping your abdominal and slightly bring the shoulders off of the mat and repeat.

# POWER PILATES PLUS EXERCISES

## Side Kick (Up and Down):

***Emphasis*** - *Works your hips, glutes, and outer thighs, while stretching your inner thighs.*

**A** Lie on your side, with your hand propped under your head. The opposite hand should rest on the floor for stability. Your hips and legs are parallel to the floor, while your feet are at an angle (partial tripod).

Inhale. Raise your top leg at a 90-degree angle, extend your leg as high as you can without bending the knee (do not lock the knee), extend the leg long.

**B** Exhale. Lower the leg back on top of the stabilized leg.

Inhale. Repeat exercise 6 times.

## Challenge:

Rest your arm on your hip and thigh instead of placing the hand in front for stability. This move works best if you have mastered the first level.

# POWER PILATES PLUS EXERCISES

## Side Kick (Front and Back):

*Emphasis - Helps to strengthen and stretch hamstrings, firm your glutes.*

**A** Lie on your side, with your head propped on your hand. The opposite hand should rest on the floor for stability. Your hips and legs are parallel to the floor, while your feet are at an angle (partial tripod).

REMEMBER - keep your navel pulled in to your spine.

**B** Inhale. Point your toes, extend your leg, kick forward and pulse twice.

Exhale. Extend leg long and extend to the back, (slow and controlled movements).

**C** Inhale. Flex your foot, extend your leg, kick forward and pulse twice.

Exhale. Extend leg long and extend to the back.

Repeat exercise 6 times on each leg.

### Challenge:
Place your hands behind your head, anchor the resting elbow on the floor; proceed with the sidekick.

# POWER PILATES PLUS EXERCISES

## Side Kick (Side Passé):

*Emphasis* - *Tones and strengthens the inner and outer thighs.*

**A** Lie on your side, with your head propped on your hand. The opposite hand should rest on the floor for stability. Your hips and legs are parallel to the floor, while your feet are at an angle (partial tripod).

Inhale. Raise your top leg at a 90-degree angle, (extend your leg as high as you can without bending the knee - extend the leg long).

**B** Exhale. Bend the knee with your toes pointing toward the ankle, extend your leg and slide it down the other extended leg.

**C** NOTE: Exhalation continues. Make sure that you complete this move with control and balance as you continue back to the starting position.

Repeat this exercise 6 times on each leg.

## Challenge:

Place your hands behind your head, anchor the resting elbow on the floor; proceed with the side kick.

# POWER PILATES PLUS EXERCISES

**A** Lie on your back with your arms extended over your head, place your legs together, feet are in the tripod stance position. Visualize yourself rolling up, by using your core.

## The Roll Up:

*Emphasis - Strengthens the lower back and abdominal muscles, stretches the hamstrings.*

**B** Inhale. Lift your head and bring your chin to your chest. Lift your arms over your head towards the ceiling and begin to roll up to a seated position, (keeping your navel pulled to your spine).

Exhale. Extend and reach your arms towards your toes (rounding your back).

**C** Inhale. Slightly round your back, and begin to roll back (arms are extended in front), then towards the ceiling and down to the starting position.

Exhale. Rest in the starting position.

Repeat this exercise 10 times.

### Modification:

If you are unable to roll up with your legs extended, bend your knees, place each hand on each thigh - bring your chin to chest and try to roll up. Roll back down using the same method.

# POWER PILATES PLUS EXERCISES

## Single Leg Stretch:

**Emphasis** - *Strengthens and elongates your legs as you work your core – while your upper body remains in a controlled position.*

**A** Lie on your back, bring one knee towards your chest, as you lengthen the other leg at a 90-degree angle. Place your outside hand on the knee, and place the other hand on the knee.

Inhale. Extend the opposite leg.

**B** Exhale. Switch legs, inhale, switch again.

Repeat this exercise 6 times on each leg.

### Challenge:
Lower your extended leg to a 45-degree angle. Place your outside hand on the ankle, and the other hand on the knee, (use controlled, fluid moves).

# POWER PILATES PLUS EXERCISES

## Teaser:

***Emphasis*** - *Improves your balance and control, coordination, works your abdominal.*

**A**   Lie on your back with your arms and legs extended at a 45-degree angle - keep your navel to your spine.

Inhale. Extend your arms forward toward your toes. Hold the V-like position, while balancing on your tailbone.

**B**   Exhale. Slowly roll back imprinting your body on to the mat.

Repeat exercise 6 times.

### Challenge:
Inhale. Balance in the V-position, (inhale) and lift your legs, (exhale) and lower your legs.

# POWER PILATES PLUS EXERCISES

## The Leg Pull:

***Emphasis -*** *Tones the glutes, and arms, stretches the hamstrings, and strengthens shoulders.*

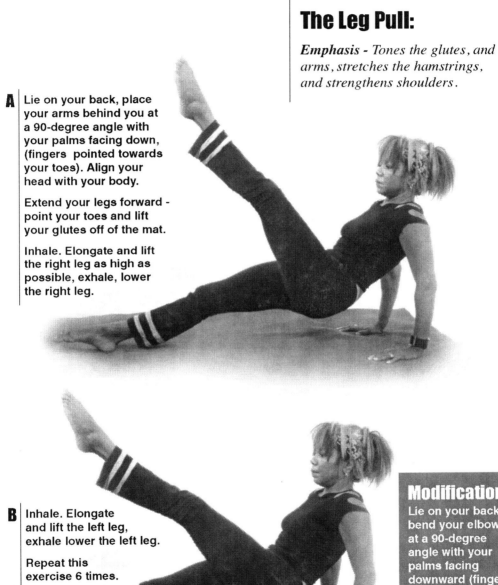

**A** Lie on your back, place your arms behind you at a 90-degree angle with your palms facing down, (fingers pointed towards your toes). Align your head with your body.

Extend your legs forward - point your toes and lift your glutes off of the mat.

Inhale. Elongate and lift the right leg as high as possible, exhale, lower the right leg.

**B** Inhale. Elongate and lift the left leg, exhale lower the left leg.

Repeat this exercise 6 times.

## Modification:

Lie on your back, bend your elbows at a 90-degree angle with your palms facing downward (fingers pointed towards your toes). This move will help you strengthen your shoulders until you are ready for the challenge pose.

# POWER PILATES PLUS EXERCISES

## The Leg Pull (Down):

*Emphasis - Strengthens the core, stretches the tendons and calves.*

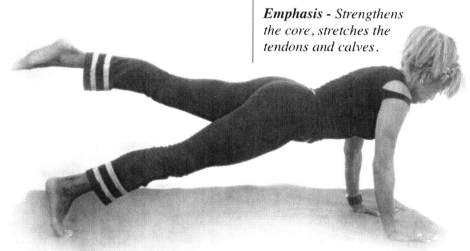

**A** Lie on your stomach, bring your body to a push up position (fingers directly under your shoulders.) Arms and legs are completely straight. Your head should be aligned with your body. Keep your core rigid and your back straight.

Inhale. Lift your right leg straight up behind you - (toes pointed).

**B** Exhale, while lowering your right leg, repeat.

Repeat this exercise 3-6 times each leg.

### Modification:
Lie on your stomach, use your forearms to push your body upwards, until you become stronger.

# POWER PILATES PLUS EXERCISES

## Single Leg Kicks:

*Emphasis - Works your hamstrings, biceps/triceps, stretches your quad and abdominal.*

**A** Lie on your stomach, lift your chest up and away from the mat with your elbows, (place your hands knuckle to knuckle) while pressing your pelvic bone into the mat. Maintain a long neck, while keeping your knees and thighs anchored to the mat.

Inhale. Raise both feet from the mat.

**B** Exhale. Kick your left foot towards your glutes, (pulsing 2 times), lower the left foot to the mat.

**C** Inhale. Kick your right foot towards your glutes, (pulsing 2 times), and lower the right foot to the mat.

Repeat this exercise 6 times each leg.

## Modification:
Imprint your upper body to the mat, and work the legs only.

# POWER PILATES PLUS EXERCISES

## A Piece of Heaven Stretch:

**Emphasis** - *Stretches and relaxes the lower back.*

**A** Place your hands and knees on the mat, (knees should be hip width, hands should be spread shoulder width), sit back on your heels.

Inhale. Bend forward. Exhale. Place your head down towards your knees, extend your arms long. Hold the position for a few seconds.

**B** Inhale. Push your body back to an upright position. Exhale. Sit back on your heels, inhale, bend forward and extend your arms long.

Repeat this stretch as needed (between exercises) 3-6 times.

**Modification:**
If you have knee or lower back problems, omit this move.

## PILATES VS. CONVENTIONAL EXERCISES

Pilates builds long and flexible muscles where conventional workouts tend to build short and bulky muscles. Pilates elongates and strengthens, while developing muscle elasticity and joint mobility.

In conventional workouts, weak muscles get weaker and strong muscles tend to get stronger, resulting in muscular imbalance. Pilates conditions the whole body, even the ankles and feet. No muscle group is over-trained or under-trained. Your entire muscular system is evenly balanced and conditioned, allowing you to enjoy daily activities and sports with greater ease and less chance of injury.

Pilates trains several muscle groups at once, in smooth, continuous movements. Using this technique, you can actually retrain your body to move in safer, more efficient patterns of motions. This technique is invaluable for sports injury recovery, sports performance, and optimal health.

Be grateful to your body for bringing you this far in life. Pilates will bring forth the power that still lies within you. These movements are designed to work your powerhouse muscles - abs, lower back, thighs, and glutes (buttocks), strengthening one muscle while stretching another.

## STARTING A PILATES PROGRAM

I always suggest that beginners start in a **Pilates Principles Class**. This class will help you understand the principles of Pilates, and ensure that you have a basic concept of the over-all philosophy of the mind and body integration fitness program. You will learn how to integrate breathing, coordination, concentration, balance, and fluidity of the movements.

**Beginner Mat Program**. After the principles are covered, you will then be introduced to a series of modified mat exercises that will help you to fully understand the movement concepts of Pilates to help you achieve the results you want.

**Intermediate and Advanced Pilates** . Once you have the basic understanding of the Pilates principles, and have mastered the beginning and modified moves with the movements becoming much easier, it is time to move to the next Pilates levels. As you graduate to the intermediate and advanced moves, you should have the ability to stabilize your pelvis while integrating more challenging moves to your Pilates sessions. At this level of you may want to integrate weights, elastic bands or other fitness accessories that will enhance your program.

**Mixed Pilates** - All Pilates levels work out together. If you are participating in this class, you will be expected to know how to work at your own level, adding modifications when you deem necessary. This class usually moves at a faster pace than a beginning class, and it offers more challenging movements.

**Golf Mat Pilates**. This class is designed to help improve core strength, flexibility, balance and stability. The benefits can work wonders for your golf game: Because you will gain more core strength, flexibility and stabilization, your golf game will improve in hitting the ball if you are not a consistent hitter, hit farther if you are, straighter and more accurately

**Prenatal and Postpartum Pilates** - Whether you are in the beginning stages of your pregnancy, trying to fit back into your pre-pregnancy clothing, or helping improve postpartum recovery, these classes are wonderful for strengthening your upper body, while relieving back pain. Some of these classes encourage new moms to bring their newborns to class! What better way to gain strength, get in great shape, and bond with your new bundle of joy?

## *PILATES APPARATUS*

**If you are up to the challenge after mastering the beginner, intermediate, and advanced Pilates moves, you may be ready for the next level - the Pilates Apparatus.**

The **Mat Bench** sits a few inches off of the floor and includes both a strap to anchor the feet, and a hand bench. It is used for the sequence of floor exercises developed by Joseph Pilates. The bench helps to strengthen and stretch the body while aligning the spine.

The **Reformer** is the most popular apparatus and is used to provide a total body workout by using springs as resistance. It's a bed-like apparatus that sits low to the floor and looks like a doorframe.

The **Cadillac** is a bed-like table that has several springs and a trapeze suspended from the top for performing full body moves.

The **Wunda Chair** is an advanced apparatus that works the body in motion, giving it a total workout; it helps develop strength, control, coordination, and balance in the body.

The **Ladder Barrel** is a padded apparatus that looks like a barrel and is used mostly to stretch and strengthen the spine.

The **Spine Corrector** is a lightweight padded apparatus that looks like a small barrel, and is used to work the abdominal muscles to help correct posture.

The ***Magic Circle*** is a padded low-resistance apparatus that is shaped in the form of a circle and is used to work the inner thighs and arm muscles.

Note: To ensure that you are using your Pilates apparatus properly, please seek the help of a knowledgeable fitness professional to get safety tips and learn how to use your machine correctly for an effective and enjoyable workout.

## *YOGA FOR EVERYONE*

In our daily chaotic, fast-paced world, most people suffer from depression, anxiety, and other stress-related disorders. Yoga benefits its practitioners mentally by offering a safe haven: a place to relax their minds, and take time to focus only on themselves and their goals. The deep breathing exercises counteract some of the physical signs of stress by decreasing the heart rate and releasing muscle tension. In addition, Yoga practice can help develop long, strong muscles, a flat stomach, a strong back, and improved posture. (Note: The art of Yoga is considered a practice because the movements and positions are just that - practice.)

Misconceptions about Yoga run rampant. At the top of the list is the belief that you need to be flexible enough able to bend and twist your body into the shape of a pretzel in order to participate in a Yoga class. Quite the contrary, you need to go to the class in order to become more flexible. Some people are concerned about their physical appearance, when it really doesn't matter what their body looks like. What matters most is how you feel while you are practicing Yoga poses. It is a practice of uniting mind, body, and spirit through physical postures, breathing exercises, and meditation.

The mind and body discipline of Yoga attracts all cultures and can be enjoyed by everyone, including those who may be limited in physical activity due to age, body shape and size, disability, or chronic illness. It can be started at any age and continued throughout life. Yoga provides a mind-body awareness that can leave your body feeling energized and relaxed. In just a few minutes a day you can alleviate stress, increase concentration, replenish, and conserve your energy levels. The gentle movements of Yoga are suitable for those of us of all ages who want to increase our productivity and inner peace, and for those who just want to be healthier and feel more relaxed.

Yoga provides maintenance for the entire body's energy systems. Simply put; Yoga provides harmony through centering, balance, and breathing. The word 'Yoga' comes from the Sanskrit root YUJ, which means to yoke, unite, join, harmonize, and blend. The art of centering, balancing, and breathing dates back thousands of years. Yoga is an ancient science dedicated to health, mind, and emotional well being. Best known as a set of physical practices, Yoga includes gentle stretches, breathing practices, and progressive deep relaxation.

Contrary to some beliefs, Yoga is not a religion, nor does it offer magical results. Although not every Yoga practitioner subscribes to a particular spiritual belief through meditation, practitioners have the opportunity to reflect on the spiritual side of life, while getting in touch with themselves and the universe. There is no secret road to super-human powers. If the powers of stretching and flexibility seem super-human, it is only because we do not realize our own potential. Yoga is designed to help the practitioner grow both physically and spiritually, and is practiced as a spiritual walkway for some, and as a gentle form of exercise for others.

Yoga is called a practice because the gentle mind and body movements are non-competitive, and offers continued growth as each person learns self-awareness, their physical limitations, and the over-all purpose of the practice. Offering more than stretching, strengthening, stress reduction, and relaxation, regular Yoga practice provides a continued mode of improvement for your physical and spiritual techniques for achieving balance within yourself, your surroundings, and others.

Note: Yoga is another form of exercise to help keep your body agile and feeling good, but it is essential to continue weight bearing, strength, and endurance exercises to achieve a well-balanced fitness program.

# YOGA

## Good Morning Body Wake-Ups

*Have* you ever noticed how cats and dogs stretch after waking from a short nap or a long nights sleep? Their movements are usually quite slow until they have performed a stretching maneuver of "downward dog" or "cat stretch" (front paws are extended as far forward as they can stretch them and their butt is pushed high into the air, while arching the back). Whatever the move, humans can certainly learn a lot from our domestic pets about stretching and getting the muscles ready for movement.

*Whether* you want to build your strength, increase your flexibility, or create long and lean muscles, you will need to get the blood circulating by going through a segment of stretching movements. The purpose of the body wake-up stretches is to warm up the muscles and prepare them for repetitive movements, while getting your circulation going. Before starting your stretching regiment, focus on centering and concentrating on the calming effect of uniting your mind and body to create a serene balance throughout your day.

*The* benefits of Yoga offer unlimited possibilities: improves muscle strength, helps improve your posture, decreases stress, and improves mental clarity. Find a branch of Yoga that works for you and stick with it, you will be amazed at the body results, inside and out.

*Breathing.* Earlier in the book I discussed different forms of breathing. For Yoga, I recommend breathing through the nose. Using the controlled breathing method, inhale through the nose and exhale through the nose. You will need to breathe deeper and exhale slower than you would an ordinary exhale. This technique will take time to master, do not be discouraged if you feel a bit lightheaded at first (if this happens, stop the controlled breathing, lie down for a few minutes and begin again). Take your time - there is no time limit to expect results, this is the reason why Yoga is called a practice. As you continue your practice your view of yourself will change for the better, while your mind, body, and spirit connect as one.

# YOGA

## Body Wake-Up Tips

• *Schedule a regular time to practice your morning body wake-ups.*

• *Ease into your stretching routine — it takes time for the body to acclimate to the new moves that are being introduced.*

• *Listen to your body — do not try to exceed your physical capacity.*

• *If you are unable to perform some of the moves, do not force your body into moves or poses that are uncomfortable.*

• *Start and finish your body wake-up stretches with a short relaxation period.*

• *Quality moves should be the focus instead of quantity moves.*

• *You should feel refreshed and energetic at the end of your body wake-up stretch.*

# YOGA BODY WAKE-UPS

**1** | Stand with your feet hip width apart, place your hands in a prayer-like position in front of your breastbone.

Close your eyes. Inhale through your nose and exhale through your nose.

**2** | Inhale. Raise both arms over your head, (arms should be shoulder width) palms are facing each other.

**3** | Exhale. Bend from the hips, slightly bending your knees, placing your hands on the floor.

## Modification:
Yoga body wake-ups can be performed by using a kneeling position, until you build up enough strength to use the standing format.

# YOGA BODY WAKE-UPS

**4** Inhale. Bend your right knee and step your left foot back into a traditional lunge pose.

(CAUTION: check to make sure that your right knee is aligned with your ankle - if your knee is extended over your ankle, you will need to make a wider stance).

**5** Exhale. Step your right foot back next to the left foot going into a push-up position.

# YOGA BODY WAKE-UPS

**6** | Inhale. Hold your push-up position for a few seconds.

**7** | Exhale. Lower your knees back to the mat from the push-up position, your chin and chest should meet the floor.

**8** | Inhale. Place your hand in front of your shoulders, bringing your chest forward and up away from the mat.

Arch your back slightly.

# YOGA BODY WAKE-UPS

**9** Exhale. Sit back on your heels, sit as tall as possible, holding your stomach in towards your spine (navel to spine).

Inhale. Extend your arms in front of you, exhale as you bend forward from the hips and slide your hands along the mat as far as you can.

**10** Inhale. Slide your hands back until they are directly under your shoulders, exhale (your knees are still hip width apart). Inhale as you arch your back.

Hold the pose for a few seconds.

**11** Exhale. Round your back, hold the pose for a few seconds.

# YOGA BODY WAKE-UPS

**12** Inhale. Slide your hands back towards your knees.

Exhale. Round your back from this position.

**13** Inhale. Place your hands under your shoulders.

Exhale. Walk your hands back towards your feet (pushing your hips towards the sky).

**14** Inhale. Step your right foot forward between your hands (look straight ahead).

Exhale. Align your left foot with the right.

# YOGA BODY WAKE-UPS

**15** Inhale. Place your hands on your shins and let your hands glide upwards along your thighs, finally landing in front of your body.

Exhale.

**16** Inhale. Raise your hands above your head (palms facing each other).

# YOGA BODY WAKE-UPS

**17** | Exhale. Begin to lower your arms and place your hands back in the prayer position.

**18** | Inhale. Stand with your feet together and hands in prayer position.

Exhale.

You are now ready to start your day.

## *FIND A COMPATIBLE YOGA PRACTICE*

All you need to do is find a simple Yoga practice that feels right for your body, create a mindset and then slip into a mental and physical refresher. For example, if you work at a desk most of the time, you can revitalize and stimulate by stretching your legs and back. There are simple Yoga movements that can help you under any circumstance, and they can be modified to fit any physical constraints. If you are currently a regular exerciser but have not found a balanced fitness program, Yoga is a good place to start.

If you are a regular exerciser, Yoga will certainly enhance your current activity by elongating your muscles, helping your joints move freely, and offer a form of deep rejuvenation that most other forms of exercise do not provide. Finally, if you are an athlete, Yoga is an absolute must to help prevent injuries, and counteract the muscular imbalances that often develop as a result of over-use or specialized training.

## *FINDING TIME FOR YOGA*

Most people believe there is no room in their busy schedule to fit another activity into their lifestyle. Actually, a full activity schedule is helpful because it will help cultivate characteristics necessary to the development and maintenance of Yoga practice. You may not have the time to practice a full Yoga sequence when you need it; however, Yoga is not limited to a regimented time schedule, a rigid, defined space, or a sequence of postures.

Before exercise, Yoga prepares your body to absorb the stress of movement by helping your muscles flex with the activity instead of tighten against it. For example, if you plan to do an aerobic workout, you should do about ten minutes of Yoga before and after your workout. The same would apply for bicycling, running, and even weight lifting.

The gentle body movements of Yoga helps prepare your mental state so you can focus on your workout. Afterwards, Yoga helps balance the muscles that were over or under-used during exercise. By neutralizing the muscle tendency to contract and become inflexible, this muscle-balancing act will help in the prevention of future injuries. Finally, Yoga encourages the flushing of lactic acid, helping your body recover from the workout more quickly.

No matter what form of exercise you decide to participate in, Yoga can make a big difference in your success with it. One of the best things about Yoga is that anyone can benefit from it; young, old, man, woman, or child. Yoga practice can increase your vitality, and reduce stress in the workplace. Overcoming stress and fatigue also helps keep you young by delaying many signs of aging.

## YOGA PATHS

There are many disciplines of Yoga that offer many methods to help you achieve your own specific goals. Seek and discover which of the many forms will work for you. The Yoga paths listed are some of the most popular disciplines, but there is no form of exercise that can extend your life, and Yoga is no exception. However, it can put the quality of life back in the years you live on this earth.

**Hatha Yoga.** Most of the Yoga practiced in Western culture falls under the broad category of Hatha Yoga. Usually, when people begin taking a Yoga class, it means that they are learning the poses and breathing techniques of Hatha Yoga. Each of the following Yoga practices shares roots in Hatha Yoga, with a common focus on awareness, conscious breathing and relaxation, and yet each one is unique.

**Astanga Yoga.** This is one of the most vigorous and dynamic paths that focuses on master control of the body. The fast-paced poses are geared to strength and flexibility improvement, with the added benefit of releasing toxins from the body as one moves through the intense workout. Fitness buffs that practice sports such as running, hiking, cycling, golf, baseball, football, and basketball all benefit tremendously from this form of Yoga. This practice is not recommended for beginners. (Note: Power Yoga is a modified version of Astanga Yoga.)

**Iyenger Yoga.** Concentrating on detail and precision of body alignment of postures, this branch of Yoga uses a variety of props like blankets, bolsters, chairs, blocks, straps, etc. The goal is to reduce stress and anxiety by placing more emphasis on posture, and less emphasis on the goals. Iyenger Yoga is recommended for beginners who welcome assistance with poses that are more challenging.

**Bikram Yoga.** Currently one of the most popular in the fitness world. This Yoga path focuses on twenty-six poses that are always repeated in the same order, and often performed in a heated room (80 to 100 degrees) to simulate the climate of India. The goal when practicing Bikram Yoga is to stretch the muscles, ligaments, and tendons, All levels, from beginners to experienced athletes, are encouraged to try this unique form of Yoga. Benefits include improved circulation, increased strength, improved flexibility, and reduced stress. Bikram Yoga is recommended for fitness enthusiasts who like action-packed high endurance fitness routines.

**Kundalini Yoga.** This Yoga path involves breathing, coordination of movement, and meditation. It stimulates the immune system, while improving strength and flexibility. Known as the Yoga of awareness, it attracts people of all ages, and those with physical limitations.

**Sivananda Yoga.** This is one of the largest disciplines in the world because it is a collective practice of postures, breathing, dietary restrictions, chanting, scriptural study, and meditation. If you are a beginner seeking a spiritual boost through chanting and meditation... then the Sivananda path awaits your participation.

**Kripalu Yoga**. Offering a three-stage practice, this form of Yoga focuses on coordinating breath, breathing, and body alignment. Practitioners often combine light, vibration, and sound with concentration, posture, and breathing. In stage one, the posture of coordination of breath and movements are emphasized, while the postures are held for short periods only. In stage two, holding and maintaining the poses for extended periods of time are called the 'process of mental purification through meditation' because the practitioner is able to access the deepest levels of the unconscious mind. In the third and final stage, the postures include spontaneous motion, and learning how to meditate while the body is in motion (when the coordination of breath, movement, and meditation become one).

## YOGA AND WEIGHT LOSS

Yoga is more than strengthening and stretching. It goes well beyond the physical and engages the mental and emotional components of well being. If you, at any time in your life have attempted weight loss, you know it is much more than counting calories, especially if you want to enjoy the process and get healthy along the way.

Yoga can help you deal with weight issues as well as the stress of daily life. It is a practice of uniting mind, body, and spirit through physical postures, breathing exercises, and meditation. Incorporating a Yoga practice into your weight loss program will improve your flexibility and strengthen and tone your muscles quickly, as your mind and body work together in unison and harmony.

When the body and the mind are united, you will make healthier food choices, select the appropriate physical activities to participate in, as well as choose people to surround yourself with who will encourage you along your journey.

## POWER YOGA

Power up your Yoga with a robust cardio activity called 'Power Yoga'. The deep, energizing breaths combined with movement and challenging poses can help train your heart and lungs, tone and sculpt your body. You can create a leaner body with this strengthening, lengthening, and effective calorie burning routine. Over 15 million Americans (twice as many as five years ago) have realized what an incredible workout one can get from Power Yoga.

**Power Yoga** differs from Ashtanga Yoga (a discipline that combines stretching, strength training, and meditation breathing). Power Yoga offers fluid movements from one pose to the next, elevates your heart rate, and improves your cardiovascular fitness, while improving flexibility and balance.

Compared to hoisting a barbell above your head, Power Yoga feels intense because you are exercising several major muscle groups simultaneously, while also stretching the opposing muscles. In just a few short minutes you will be sweating like a steam pipe, and in a matter of months, you will notice improvement in both strength and flexibility. Continue this routine and your body will look sleek, toned, and well proportioned from head to toe.

Power Yoga links the body and breath as one. The warm-up begins by moving through a sequence of slow, methodical moves. This process helps warm all the muscles of body, preparing the large, as well as the smaller muscles, for increased flexibility and improved balance. The cardio workout gives participants an opportunity to get their heart rates up, which yields some wonderful cardio benefits. Many of the poses resemble basic calisthenics, push-ups, handstands, toe touches, and side bends. The essence of Power Yoga is sweat producing, while muscle building at a constant pace. There are no breaks as the body movements flow one right into the next, making it an intense aerobic workout. Try to do at least 30 minutes of cardio activity 3 to 5 times a week. (Note: While this workout will get your heart rate up and yield some cardiovascular benefits, it should not be substituted for a regular aerobic workout program)

Power Yoga is becoming quite popular and many health clubs have added classes to their weekly schedules. Costs vary, but you can expect to pay $8 to $15 for an hour-long class. You do not need additional equipment, but you will need to wear loose fitting clothing or spandex. It is essential to drink water before *and* after your class, because you will perspire, and heavily at times.

Caution: Beginners should ease into Power Yoga gradually, never stretching to the point of pain. Power Yoga involves twisting and weight bearing moves; use precaution if you have a history of neck, back, shoulder, and/or knee injuries.

Final thoughts on Power Yoga: Relax, and let your mind and body engage in this wonderful form of body integration.

## *NEVER TOO LATE TO STRETCH - YOGA AND AGING*

The accepted view of the aging process is stiffening of the joints, rigidity, and the body shutting down. If the body does not have proper exercise, it loses height and strength flexibility. As we grow older, our muscles and joints tighten and stiffen, often causing discomfort and anxiety, affecting our over-all well being. Sometimes this results in our natural ability to perform simple day-to-day activities being restricted, or even worse.

Yoga helps reverse the aging process by moving each joint in the body through its full range of motion through stretching, strengthening, and balancing each body part. The effective movements, breathing techniques, and relaxation exercises offer many benefits: improved muscle tone, stronger bones, greater range of motion and flexibility, greater lung capacity and ease of breathing, improved balance, and a higher energy level.

Whatever your motivation is for practicing Yoga - losing weight, strengthening your body, gaining more flexibility, or relieving stress, the powerful mind and body connection poses can bring tremendous results, while creating a new outlook about your mind and body.

Because diverse groups of people are attracted to Yoga, everyone (seated or standing) can enjoy the mind and body principles, including those who may be physically limited because of age, body shape and size, disability, or chronic illness. The key factors to starting a Yoga program safely is to move slowly, know your physical limitations, and have a knowledgeable instructor. A good teacher will be able to help you adapt challenging poses to your physical ability and fitness level. Remember to talk to your doctor first if you have an injury or a health condition that may be of concern.

Whether you choose the ever-popular mind and body conditioning of Pilates or Yoga, the ancient art form is recognized worldwide, and is known for the most effective forms of exercise for the body, as well as relaxation for the mind and spirit. Mind-body fitness offers unlimited possibilities.

The concepts of Pilates and Yoga are not outcomes, but continuous journeys. There are no goals; only the will to better one's self, which will lead to a wonderful sense of well being

## *WHAT YOU SHOULD DO BEFORE STARTING A YOGA CLASS*

Find a class that suits your needs. Look for classes that are billed 'Gentle' or 'Easy'. Classes are offered in many locations: YMCAs, health clubs, Senior and community centers. Most classes last anywhere from 60 to 90 minutes per session.

Do not eat a large meal or drink a lot of water before class. Ideally, your stomach should be 1/2 full of food, 1/4 full of water, and the remaining 1/4 empty for breathing. (Wait 15 to 20 minutes after a Yoga workout before eating.)

Arrive at your class early, and alert the instructor about your beginner status. Position yourself where you can easily see and hear the Instructor.

Listen to your body and be realistic of your physical ability. You will want to push yourself so you are doing the work; however, you do not want to hurt yourself. Also, avoid wiping the sweat from your body after a workout; instead dab, or rub the moisture (and lost minerals) back into the skin to be reabsorbed.


## *YOGA PROPS*

For those of you who are interested in taking your practice to a new challenge level, I have included a list of Yoga props that are commonly used for enhancement. Many Yoga teachers work with Yoga props because they aid in the effectiveness of learning and practicing Yoga postures.

**Yoga Mats**. Often referred to as 'sticky' mats, these mats are made to be non-slippery on the floor while providing a stable surface. Yoga mats come in many colors and heights, and may be rolled up, or folded easily for travel.

**Straps or Belts**. Straps can be used for multiple purposes; helping extend your reach, opening your shoulders and hips, maintaining length and evenness in your arms and legs all the while encouraging you to move deeper over-all into many Yoga poses.

**Sand Bags**. Used as soft, gentle weights, sandbags encourage the body to release beneath their weight, thereby increasing the depths of each stretch.

**Blankets**. One of the most versatile Yoga props, blankets can be used for support in sitting poses, rolled into a bolster, folded into a shoulder stand or a headstand pad, and used as a cover during relaxation and meditation.

**Blocks**. Another versatile prop, a block is helpful as a hand rest in standing poses such as the triangle. It can also be used under the sacrum (tailbone), between the hands, and under the feet, giving the body lift and support.

**Boosters**. The booster supports and encourages your body to relax and stretch in areas that need it.

**Eye bags**. Because we often hold tension in the muscles around the eyes and in the brow, the gentle weight of an eye bag on these muscles helps them relax, and the darkness provided by the eye bag lets the pupils and eye muscles relax.

**Cushions**. Often called 'meditation cushions', they give firm support and extra height support, allowing optimum length and alignment of the spine while sitting. This encourages the hips and legs to relax by bringing lift and openness to the chest and lungs.

## OTHER MIND AND BODY TECHNIQUES

There are a variety of relaxation techniques used in mind-body activities and therapies, including massage and touch therapy.

If you would like to explore the theory and concepts of other mind and body techniques, here is a synopsis of other popular techniques:

**Nia** is an expressive fitness and awareness movement program that is filled with depth, tenderness, and clarity. Nia is considered a holistic approach to health by blending movements, concepts, and theories from a variety of cultures. This form of therapy is relatively new to the mind and body concept. This fascinating concept provides the stillness and concentration of tai-chi, the dynamic poses of Yoga, the explosive power of martial arts, and the grace and spontaneity of modern and ethnic dances, making it possible to stay fit and reap holistic benefits at the same time.

**Meditation**. People in many religious contexts have practiced meditation (mind focusing techniques) for many years. Meditation is considered an active process in which the individual is mentally alert, while being physically relaxed with the body passive. This mind-body technique is particularly used for stress reduction, as well as after physical activity.

**Martial Arts** are designed to promote mental and spiritual development, and are often known as methods of self-defense or combat. However, they are also beneficial in the development of physical fitness, as well as promoting mental and spiritual development. These highly disciplined activities are aimed at uniting the mind, body, and spirit, while bringing balance to the participant's life.

**Alexander Technique**. This technique works to help change movement habits for the better in daily life activities. This technique teaches the use of the appropriate amount of effort it takes for a particular activity; a simple and practical method for improving ease and freedom of movement, balance, support and coordination. It is not a series of treatments or exercises, but rather a re-education of the mind and body connection. The Alexander technique can help a person discover, or rediscover, a new balance in the body by releasing unnecessary tension. It can be utilized while lying down, sitting, standing, walking, lifting, and doing other daily activities.

**Tai Chi** is known as 'meditation in motion' and is closely related to Qi Gong. Both meditation and certain types of Qi Gong follow a 'top-down' approach, with the mind initiating the meditative state, or initiating the Qi flow. Tai Chi is often referred to as a 'means to return to childhood', because the internal discipline of this form of movements first trains the nervous system so the complex movements become natural and spontaneous. Tai Chi has been practiced by multiple generations of practitioners, who practice from a young age until taking their final breath.

**Qi Gong** works with the body's energy. This gentle mind and body practice is easy to follow through a combination of controlled breathing, focused concentration, and simple movement. According to the ancient Chinese model, sickness, pain, and other health problems are caused when Qi is blocked. When Qi cannot flow through the body, excess Qi builds up where it is not needed or wanted, and the body beyond the blockage does not receive enough Qi. It's like water being dammed on a river; it causes flooding in the immediate area, while depriving the area downstream of life-giving water. Qi exercises remove these blockages, and increase the flow of energy through the body. When Qi flows free, energy heals and restores the body.

**Feldenkrais** is the form of gentle movement and directed attention to improve movement and enhance human functioning. Using this method will enable you to increase your range of motion, improve flexibility and coordination, while rediscovering your innate capacity for graceful, efficient movement. Ordinarily, we learn 'just enough'. For example, we learn to use our hands well enough to eat, and our legs well enough to walk. The Feldenkrais Method teaches, through movement, how we can improve our normal daily capabilities in everyday life.

# PART IV

## *NUTRITION FACTS - TIPS & BITS*

*

## WATER - LIQUID LIFE

On a hot day nothing quenches your thirst like H2O. Water is our life support for survival. Did you know 60% of the human body is comprised of water, and it needs a steady supply to survive? Humans can live for months without solid foods, but will die in a few days without water. (The longest documented period of time for a person to go without food or water is 18 days.) Water is vital for our survival, because we cannot store or conserve it.

Most of us do not drink enough water. If asked, many people would tell you that they drink plenty of fluids every day by drinking coffee, tea, hot chocolate, etc. Some people drink other fluids such as soda, juice, and milkshakes as a substitute, but keep in mind that nothing takes the place of water. If you are not a regular water drinker, try to start a habit of drinking a glass first thing in the morning (drinking warm water first thing in the morning will gently wake up your body from the inside out). Make it a habit to drink water in the morning, throughout the day, before and after each meal, and before bedtime.

If you drink 64 ounces of water a day, 64 fluid ounces of water a day must be eliminated to maintain a proper water balance in your body. Think of drinking water as an internal shower: every time you drink, and the more water you drink, your body eliminates toxins that might otherwise linger in your system.

How much water should you drink every day? Everyone has a theory about the amount of water a person should consume daily, some say eight glasses, others say three to five glasses. Here is a formula that will get you started: drink enough water that equals one-half of your body weight (in ounces). Example: if your weight is 150 lbs., you will need to drink at least 75 ounces of water everyday, but not all at once, of course. It is vital to keep your body hydrated, especially during hot weather.

I always suggest that a person drink water throughout the day to prevent their body from going into a state of dehydration, especially during hot weather. It is important to know that the dehydration process has already started if you feel thirsty. You can usually determine your body's level of dehydration by checking the color of your urine. Urine should be a very pale yellow, almost clear. If the color is dark yellow, your body is already on its way to a state of dehydration. (There are always exceptions to the rule, since some vitamin supplements, prescription drugs, and antibiotics will cause urine to turn yellow, or even orange.)

A few words to athletes and dieters: water is critical for all the chemical reactions in the body. Dehydration can occur rapidly during workouts, so beginners and athletes need to be aware of their daily fluid intake to prevent dehydration, as well as muscle cramps during physical activity.

Before working out, drink at least eight ounces of water. During your workout, try to drink eight ounces every ten minutes, and afterwards, eight to sixteen ounces of water. Sports drinks are a good choice because they can quickly correct the ratio of your electrolyte potassium and sodium levels. By now, you know my opinion about dieting: there is no such thing as a diet - only a lifestyle change. For those people trying to lose a few pounds by cutting calories and exercising, drinking a gallon of water daily will act as a diuretic to help rid the body of excess fluid.

**Interesting facts about average daily water consumption:**

- 10% of water is gained as by-products of metabolism

- 30% comes from water in the moist foods we eat

- 60% comes from water and beverages we drink

**Interesting facts about average daily output of water:**

- 10% of water is lost through elimination (feces)

- 12% of water is lost as a result of sweating

- 31% of water loss is through the skin and lungs

- 47% of water loss is through elimination (urine)


## CARBOHYDRATES

Carbohydrates, as well as proteins and minimal fats, have always been the basis for a well-rounded diet. Even though some low-carb and no-carb diet folks have rejected them, carbohydrates are not only good for you, but are also an essential, primary source of energy for the body. Since most of us are counting carbohydrates these days, what it is that we are actually counting? Carbohydrate counting specifically measures the upward drive each meal has on blood sugar level. High-fat foods can contribute to obesity, heart disease, and higher blood sugars in the long run, but dietary fat plays only a minor role in daily blood sugar control. Protein is a minor player in short-term blood-sugar control, and over a period of several hours, half of the protein we eat is converted to carbohydrates.


## GLYCEMIC INDEX

The Glycemic Index measures just how fast a food is likely to raise your blood sugar, and can be helpful in managing your blood sugar level. For example, if your blood sugar is low and continues to drop during exercise, you should eat a high-carbohydrate food that will raise your blood sugar quickly. If you want to keep your blood sugar from dropping during a few hours of mild activity, you may prefer to eat a carbohydrate with a lower Glycemic Index, and longer action time. Better food control depends on how quickly the foods you consume raises your blood sugar.

All carbohydrates are not created equal! To control your carbohydrates, choose foods at 50 to 60 grams or below whenever possible. If you are new to a low-carbohydrate diet or a low-glycemic diet, stay below 30 grams for the first two weeks, then gradually add carbohydrates that are higher on the index, until your weight loss stops. That way, you will be able to see which carbohydrates are considered safe.

Experiment with carbohydrates, as there really is no exact science. Your food intake must be customized, because everybody reacts differently to various foods. Here are a few examples of commonly eaten foods, ranking from high to low on the Glycemic Index.

## GLYCEMIC INDEX FOODS (listed by grams per serving)

### Greater than 100 grams
Puffed rice, instant rice, French bread, corn flakes, dates

### Between 80 and 100 grams
Potatoes, oat bran, white rice, carrots, corn, raisins, pretzels, white bread, glucose.

### Between 60 and 75 grams
Bananas, bran muffins, shortbread (two cookies), shredded wheat, corn tortilla, refined pasta, and tapioca

### Between 40 and 60 grams
Brown rice, apples, pears, cheese tortellini, popcorn (2 cups), Pumpernickel bread (one slice), oatmeal (not instant), sponge cake

### Below 30 grams
lentils, green vegetables, dried apricots, cherries, yogurt, skim milk, strawberries, plums, grapefruit, prunes, peaches, peanuts, fructose

## *FIBER*

Dietary fiber is a group of complex carbohydrates that are not an energy source. The digestive enzymes cannot break the links that hold 'fiber sugar units' together. There are no calories in fiber and it cannot be converted into glucose.

The typical American diet includes a low level of fiber intake. The average woman gets 12 grams of fiber a day from food, and the average man, 17 grams. This is well below the recommended 20 to 35 grams a day, and can be a direct contributor to colon cancer, high blood pressure, and the rapid growing rate of obesity.

Dietary fiber is classified into two categories; insoluble, and soluble.

**Insoluble fiber** absorbs water, helping you feel full after eating, and stimulates your intestinal walls to contract and relax, moving solid materials through the digestive tract. You find insoluble fiber in cabbage leaves, carrots, beets, whole wheat, beans, plant stems, and seed coverings (bran, whole grains.) When food moves quickly through the intestines, the insoluble fiber helps ensure carcinogens (cancer causing substances) do not stay in contact with the bowel lining long enough to have a damaging effect. This fiber helps bulk up the stool and makes it softer, helping to eliminate the chance of constipation, and reducing the chance of developing hemorrhoids. It also eases the discomfort level if you have an existing problem.

**Soluble Fiber** helps lower the amount of cholesterol circulating in the blood. This fiber can also create a feeling of fullness without adding water. Soluble fiber is found in fruits, apples, strawberries, citrus fruits, oats, barley, beans, cereals, rice and seeds.

If you are accustomed to a low-fiber diet, be sure to increase your intake gradually. This will prevent intestinal distress, such as diarrhea, bloating, flatulence, and stomach cramps.

**Fiber content of common foods (per serving):**

Almonds: 7 grams
Apples: 2 grams
Apricots: 6 grams
Avocados: 3.5 grams
Baked beans: 4 grams
Brown rice: 1 gram
Carrots: 2.5 grams
Corn flakes: 1 gram
Dates: 5 grams
Lima beans: 7 grams
Peanuts: 6 grams
Prunes: 6 grams
Raisins: 2 grams
Spinach: 2 grams
Whole grain bread: 6 grams
Whole grain flour: 9 grams

## *PROTEIN*

Our bodies depend on protein from food for daily performance. Muscles are made of protein, and protein gives your body the right stuff to fight disease, build new cells, and maintain all types of tissue in the body.

Protein is found throughout our bodies in the form of hair, skin, and nails. Every cell in our body has protein, and different proteins perform different functions to keep the body operational. Protein is lost daily from the body through shedding of hair, skin and nails (cut, broken or trimmed), along with the protein that is routinely broken down in the body.

Some proteins are broken down into amino acids. The body arranges amino acids into different combinations, creating the various kinds of protein needed to keep the body powered up. In order to keep up with the body's requirements, you need to eat certain foods that provide the needed daily supply of amino acids. Because there are many amino acids the body can arrange and rearrange for various purposes, it is essential to get nine of the twenty amino acids from your daily diet (the body produces the remaining amino acids naturally). Red meats, chicken, fish, and other protein rich foods can help ensure you are getting enough protein in your daily diet. The quantity of protein consumption depends on individual body types and daily lifestyles.

If you exercise on a regular basis, your body requires a higher quantity of protein because the protein in the body breaks down during workouts and other muscular activities. There have been various studies showing that physically active people, athletes, runners, weightlifters, etc., fall short of consuming the recommended daily allowance of protein to meet their daily needs for sports performance.

Caution: Excessive protein consumption, five or more times the recommended daily allowance, could be hazardous to your health. It is highly possible to lose bone calcium via urine, and particularly dangerous for women who are at risk for osteoporosis. Consuming too much protein can also lead to dehydration, since most of the water we drink is utilized in excreting protein waste in the urine. In addition, eating too much protein high in fat and cholesterol should be avoided for cardiovascular health.

Here are some recommendations of protein rich foods: egg beaters, fresh tuna or salmon (broiled, baked, or grilled), garbanzo beans, grains, lean cuts of beef, lean ham and turkey, lentils, low-fat cottage cheese, non-fat yogurt, peanut butter, pinto beans, skinless chicken pieces, soy beans, and tofu.

## Daily Protein Consumption Recommendations by Body Frame:

- Petite (5'1" and shorter)
  60 to 70 grams of protein

- Small (5'2" to 5'5")
  7O to 8O grams of protein

- Medium (5'6" to 5'9")
  8O to 9O grams of protein

- Large (5'10" and taller)
  9O to 1OO grams of protein

**Note- If you exercise 3 times a week or more, add 10 additional grams of protein per day to your diet.**


## *VITAMINS AND MINERALS*


## FAT SOLUBLE VITAMINS

Fat Soluble vitamins can be stored in the body and do not need to be consumed daily. While it is difficult to 'overdose' on them from ordinary dietary sources, consuming mega doses of most fat-soluble vitamins, especially A and D, can lead to a dangerous buildup in the body. The following list below will give you a better understanding of fat soluble vitamins, their contributions to the body, and food sources where they are found:

Vitamin A: needed for the eyes, skin, and nails. It helps maintain glands, gums, bones and teeth, helps ward off infections, and helps prevent night blindness. Sources - milk products, carrots, calf's liver, apricots, cooked spinach.

Beta-carotene: facilitates cell growth, and acts as an antioxidant. Sources of beta-carotene can be found in fruits and vegetables.

Vitamin D: helps build and maintain teeth and bones, and enhances calcium absorption. Sources of this vitamin can gained from sunlight and eating eggs, fish, and drinking milk products.

Vitamin E: helps form red blood cells, muscles, and other tissues, and preserves fatty acids.
Sources of vitamin E are found in vegetable oils, nuts, greens, and wheat germ.

Vitamin K: needed for regular blood clotting, and bone metabolism. Sources of this vitamin are found in leafy green vegetables, cereals, fruits, milk products, meats, cabbage, cucumber, green beans, and cauliflower.

## WATER SOLUBLE VITAMINS

Water-soluble vitamins are not stored in our bodies and should be consumed daily. The following list will give you information about the contributions of water-soluble vitamins and the food sources where they can be found:

**Vitamin B1** (thiamine): enhances energy by promoting the metabolism of carbohydrates, promotes normal appetite and digestion, and proper nerve function. Sources of vitamin B1 are found in pork, grains, and beans.

**Vitamin B2** (riboflavin): needed for the metabolism of all foods, and the release of energy to cells. It also helps maintain our mucous membranes and vision. Sources of vitamin B2 are found in milk, eggs, fish, meat, and leafy green vegetables.

**Vitamin B3** (niacin): needed in many enzymes that convert food into energy. Promotes normal appetite, digestion, and nerve function. Large doses may lower cholesterol. Sources of vitamin B3 are found in nuts, fish, poultry, and grains.

**Vitamin B5**: needed to manufacture the adrenal hormones and chemicals that regulate nerve functions. Sources - found in most plants and animal foods.

**Vitamin B6**: needed for protein metabolism and absorption, and carbohydrate metabolism. It helps form red blood cells, and promotes nerve and brain functions. Sources of this vitamin are found in meats, grains, vegetables, and fruit.

**Vitamin B12**: helps build genetic material, and aids in forming red blood cells. Sources - meat, milk products, eggs, liver, kidney meat, fish, sauerkraut, and yogurt.

**Biotin**: needed for metabolism of glucose, and the formation of certain fatty acids, which are essential for proper body chemistry. Sources of biotin are found in beans, vegetables, and meats.

**Folic Acid**: needed in the manufacture of genetic material and red blood cells. Sources - nuts, spinach, chicken liver, cottage cheese, wheat bran, chickpeas, brussel sprouts, sunflower, peanuts, cantaloupe, and honeydew melons.

**Vitamin C**: helps bind the cells together. It also strengthens blood vessel walls, keeps gums healthy, helps the body resist infection, and promotes healing. Sources of these powerful vitamins are found in citrus fruits and vegetables.


## MINERALS

Minerals are inorganic substances that perform a variety of vital functions in the body.

The following list will give you information about the contributions of minerals to the body and food sources where they can be found:

**Calcium**: helps build strong bones and teeth, promotes muscle and nerve function, and helps with the blood's ability to clot. It also helps activate the enzymes needed to convert food into energy. Sources of calcium are found in milk products, vegetables, and legumes.

**Magnesium**: activates the enzymes needed to release energy in the body. It promotes bone growth, and is needed by cells for genetic material. Sources of magnesium are found in grains and greens.

**Phosphorus**: along with calcium builds bones and teeth. It is needed for metabolism, body chemistry, and nerve and muscle function. Sources of phosphorus can be found in milk products, meats, poultry, fish, eggs, and grains.

**Potassium**: helps regulate fluid balance. It is also needed for nerve and muscle function, and metabolism. Sources - green beans, bananas, meats, milk products, potatoes, and coffee.

## TRACE MINERALS

Trace Minerals are as essential to health as macro minerals, but are only needed in very small amounts. Following is a list of these minerals, their contributions to the body, and food sources where they are found:

**Copper**: a component of several enzymes, including one that is needed to make skin, hair, and other pigments. It stimulates iron absorption, and is needed to develop and maintain red blood cells, connective tissue, nerve fibers, and aids in wound healing. Sources can be found in meats, milk and milk products, shellfish, poultry, and water.

**Iron**: essential for making hemoglobin, the red substance in blood that carries oxygen to body cells. Sources - meats, dried fruits, nuts, beans, dark leafy green vegetables, Brussels sprouts, breads and cereals.

**Manganese**: needed for normal tendon and bone structure. It is a component of some of the enzymes that are important in metabolism. Sources - greens, blueberries, wheat bran, pineapple, coffee, tea, whole grains, cereals, and legumes.

**Selenium**: interacts with vitamin E to prevent the breakdown of fats and body chemicals. Sources - seafood, poultry, meats, grains, brown rice, and oatmeal.

**Zinc**: an element in more than 100 enzymes that is essential to digestion and metabolism. Sources of zinc include meat, poultry, fish, milk products, grains, cereals, fruits, and vegetables.

## MAINTAINING A HEALTHY IMMUNE SYSTEM

To help maintain a healthy immune system, a well balanced diet should include:

Beta-carotene: stimulates natural killer cells in the immune system, helping cells fight infections.

Folate (folic acid): essential for the growth and maintenance of cells (brewers yeast, orange juice, beets and avocados are great sources of folic acid).

Selenium: promotes action against toxic bacteria.

Vitamin B6: promotes proliferation of white blood cells, which helps fight infections.

Vitamin C: enhances the immune response.

Vitamin E: stimulates the immune response.

Zinc: promotes wound healing.

Disclaimer: This information should be used as a resource guide only. I am not a medical doctor, and the information provided above is to help inform and educate you about the many benefits of vitamins and minerals. If you believe your body may be deficient in any vitamins or minerals, check with your physician in order to pursue better health.

Note: Remember that regular physical activity has been known to bolster the immune system, whereas stress and exhaustion may impair its function by creating a vulnerable upper respiratory system, prone to infections.

## *MOST FREQUENTLY ASKED QUESTIONS ABOUT VITAMINS AND MINERALS*

Our bodies require more than 45 nutrients from the diet to maintain health. These 45+ nutrients can be obtained from a variety of foods and dietary patterns within a wide range of caloric intakes. The first step in providing the best nutrition for the body is to understand the basics of nutrients, organizing this information into a simple guideline for dietary intake, and the importance of designing a diet that provides optimal, not minimal, amounts of all vitamins and minerals.

Here are questions and answers to some of the most frequently asked questions about vitamins and minerals:

## What are nutrient dense foods?

Nutrient dense foods provide a large amount of vitamins and/or minerals for a relatively small amount of calories. Examples of nutrient dense foods include fruits and vegetables, whole grain breads and cereals, cooked dry beans and peas, low-fat or non-fat dairy products, fish, chicken without the skin, and lean meats. Foods steamed, baked, or broiled with no additional butter, margarine or other fats are also nutrient dense.

## What is a calorie?

A calorie (also known as a kilocalorie) is a measurement of energy in food. A calorie is the amount of heat energy required to raise the temperature of 1,000 grams of water by 1 degree, Celsius. Proteins and carbohydrates in food provide 4 calories/gram, whereas fats provide 9 calories/gram, and alcohol, 7 calories/grams. Vitamins and minerals do not supply calories.

## What is a calorie dense food?

A calorie dense food is one that supplies small amounts of vitamins and/or minerals and relatively large amount of calories. Calorie dense foods include high fat and high sugar foods, such as butter, oils, candy, bacon, hot dogs, cookies, and fried foods.

## What is a balanced diet?

A balanced diet is one where all vitamins, minerals, and other nutrients are supplied in optimal amounts. The typical balanced diet contains a variety of foods from the following selections: fresh fruits and vegetables, whole grain breads and cereals, cooked dried beans and peas, low-fat or non-fat dairy products, lean meats, chicken, fish, nuts, and seeds.

## What is a free radical?

Free radicals are highly reactive substances found in air pollution, tobacco smoke, rancid foods, and are produced in the body. They damage cell membranes resulting in body tissue destruction, possibly leading to disease.

## At what level does the consumption of taking vitamins become toxic?

Toxic symptoms from ingesting too many vitamins will vary on the length of time large doses are consumed, the type of vitamin consumed, and the site and possibly the age of the individual. Example: the adult RDA (recommended daily allowance) for vitamin A is 4,000 IU (International Units) for women and 5,000 for men. Vitamin A (retinol) found in fish liver oils, liver, and some supplements, can cause nausea, vomiting, joint and abdominal pain, bone abnormalities, hair loss, and liver damage in some people. Infants and children should consume no more than the RDA of 1,400 to 3,000 IU, depending on their age and gender. Regular consumption of vitamin A in amounts exceeding 10,000 IU should be done only under the supervision of a physician.

## How do I know if I am taking enough calcium?

National nutrition surveys show that many Americans are not consuming adequate amounts of calcium. One cup of non-fat or low-fat milk or yogurt, 1 1/2 ounces of low-fat cheese, 2 cups of cottage cheese, or 2 cups of broccoli provide 300 mg of calcium each. At least three servings a day of these or other calcium-rich foods (or a combination of food and other calcium sources) should be consumed to aid in the prevention of osteoporosis.

**Do senior citizens require more vitamins and minerals than their younger adult counterparts?**
Seniors are one of the more nutritionally vulnerable groups. In addition, the aging process often masks or overlaps the recognized signs of vitamin and/or mineral deficiencies. Seniors who do not take supplements often are low in vitamins A, E, C, B1, B2, B12, folic acid, calcium, selenium, and chromium.

Rule of thumb - it is always best to follow the recommendations on the vitamin or mineral bottle label. Consult with your doctor for additional instructions.

## *FOOD FACTS, NUTRITION LABELS, AND TERMINOLOGY*

Consumer friendly food labels usually include a mini nutrition guide showing the food's nutrient content and an evaluation of its place in a balanced diet, an ingredients listing in a decreasing order based on the quantity of each ingredient in the food, and scientific information about the relationship between certain foods and specific health conditions such as heart disease and cancer.

Labels now list fourteen nutrients, including fat, fiber, and protein, and the terms 'light' and 'reduced' have been clearly defined. Nutritional serving sizes have been defined, and grocery store bins now display the listings of nutritional value of fresh foods like fruits, vegetables, and seafood.

**Serving Size** (a serving size is usually ½ cup). If the normal serving size is the same size as the one given on the label, and you eat double the serving size, you will need to double the nutrient values when calculating your caloric intake.

**Total Fat** - the acceptable amount of fat varies for each food group, the lower the fat content, the better it is for you.

**Saturated Fat** - most of the saturated fat in your diet should come from meat, poultry, and dairy foods, (not processed foods). Avoid foods with high saturated fat numbers.

**Cholesterol** - found only in animal products. Meats, fish, poultry, and high fat dairy products contain it. A limit of 300 mg or less per day is recommended.

**Sodium** - it is important to restrict the amount of sodium in the diet. No more than 2000 mg of sodium should be included in the daily diet.

Avoid foods that contain the following saturated fats: animal fat, bacon, beef fat, beef tallow, butter, cheese, chicken fat, chocolate, coca butter, coconut cream, coconut oil, hydrogenated fat/oil, lard, palm kernel oil, palm oil, salt pork, sour cream, and whole milk.

## FOOD LABEL TERMINOLOGY

Listed below are definitions of some of the most commonly used terms on food labels:

**Aspartame** - (artificial sweetener) such as Equal and Nutrasweet.

**Calorie** (1/1000 of a kilocalorie) - a calorie gives the body the ability to metabolize, or burn food to produce energy in the form of heat that warms the body and powers every movement. A calorie is as important to the body as gasoline is to an automobile.

**Calorie free** - fewer than five calories per serving.

**Cholesterol free** - means less than five milligrams of cholesterol, or two grams or less of saturated fat per serving.

**Egg Substitutes** - varies from manufacturer to manufacturer. Comprised of egg whites with food coloring added (to emulate the sunny yellow of beaten eggs), with gums and other stabilizers blended together to create an approximate texture. Note: some egg substitutes contain fat, others none at all. Read the food label carefully before making your purchase.

**Emulsifier** - a category of additives used in processed foods whose function is to keep oil and water, or other nonfat liquid, from separating, keeping them smoothly blended.

**Enriched** - when wheat is milled into white flour, or refined into breads and cereals, it loses iron, the B complex vitamins, thiamin, bioflavin, and niacin. The milling and refining process also destroys fiber, vitamin B6, zinc, magnesium, and other trace minerals. Replacing these items back into the wheat product is the enriching process. (Whole grain is still the healthiest option.)

**Extra lean** - a 3½ ounce (100 grams) portion of meat, game, fowl, or seafood containing less than 5 grams of fat (2 grams saturated) and 94 milligrams cholesterol.

**Fat free** - a serving size must not exceed 5 calories, 5 milligrams sodium, 2 milligrams cholesterol, or ½ gram each of sugar, fat, and saturated fat.

**FDA** - Food and Drug Administration.

**Free** - means negligible measurement.

**Fresh** - food that has never been heated, frozen, or pasteurized.

**Fresh frozen** - fresh foods that may or may not have been blanched before being frozen. Good source of fiber - 2.5 to 4.9 grams per serving.

**High fiber** - 5 grams or more per serving.

**Homogenized** - oil and non-oily liquids that are blended together at an intense speed until the two are smooth and creamy. Milk is forced through grids of tiny holes under 2000 to 2500 pounds of pressure so its fat particles are reduced to a smooth consistency that keeps the fat from separating out. Many of the salad dressings we use today have been homogenized.

**Lean** (same as extra lean) - meats, game, fowl, or seafood cannot contain more than 10 grams of fat (4 grams saturated)

**Less** - contains 25% fewer calories.

**Lite** - food in which the calories have been reduced by one-third, and the fat by one-half.

**Low** - a serving size of 1¾ ounces (50 grams) must not exceed 40 calories, 140 milligrams sodium, or 3 grams fat (1 gram saturated). Quantities of low cholesterol foods cannot exceed more than 20 milligrams of cholesterol.

**Organic foods** - foods untouched by synthetic fertilizers, pesticides, herbicides, artificial preservatives or additives.

**RDA** - Recommended Daily Allowance

**Reduced** - food in which calories, or a particular nutrient, has been reduced by 25%.

**Serving size** - most nutritionists and athletes agree that the following proportion sizes are adequate for a healthy person for one meal: 2 to 3 ounces meat, fish or poultry; ½ cup fruits and vegetables; 8 ounces milk; 1 slice bread or 1 ounce of cereal. Note: the number of proportions will depend on age, gender, and lifestyle (jock or couch potato). A healthy meal consists of portions and servings that meet the daily food requirements for fat, proteins, carbohydrates, vitamins, and minerals.

**Soymilk** - milky substance extracted from fresh pureed soybeans that is often used in place of animal milk.

**Trace minerals** - minerals needed by the body in limited amounts that helps the body burn fuel, helps shuttle oxygen to red blood cells, and are a component of proteins and nucleic acids.

**Sugar free** - contains less than a gram of sugar per standard serving size.

**USDA** - United States Department of Agriculture. An important federal agency that develops markets to boost farm income, and works to stamp out hunger and malnutrition. This agency conducts nutritional research and sets standards on grading meats, eggs, dairy products, fruits, and vegetables.

**USRDA** - United States Recommended Daily Allowance. The Food and Drug Administration developed recommendations from the Food and Nutrition Board guidelines for use in labeling foods. Effective in 1990, the USRDA were replaced by Reference Daily Intakes (RDI)
Vegetable gums - plant extracts used by food processors to thicken, smooth, and stabilize puddings, frozen desserts, and salad dressings.

**Whey** - milky liquid left after milk or cream has curded. There are sweet and sour wheys; sweet whey is used to curd milk for cheddar and Swiss cheeses. Sour whey is a by-product of cottage cheese manufacturing. Whey is a good source of milk sugar and proteins, and should not be thrown away.

**Zinc** - the body cannot function without this heavy metal. The body needs zinc to metabolize carbohydrates, fats, proteins, and alcohol. Zinc helps build the immune system, and also helps wounds heal faster.

Keeping track of all of these nutritional facts can boggle the mind, but it is necessary to keep your dietary habits balanced and in check.

## YOU ARE WHAT YOU EAT!

### *POWER FOODS - FOOD ENERGIZERS*

Get energized! Energy foods help maximize our mental performance and our ability to cope with stress under pressure, making us less prone to depression, headaches, and over-all tiredness.

Start your day off right. Sharpen your mental clarity and physical performance by starting your day off with a power packed, high-energy, low sugar breakfast. You can then boost your vitality level at mid-morning by treating yourself to a light snack. Maintain a regular schedule for meal times, and try not to skip meals because it can slow your metabolic rate down. Whenever possible, include salads, green leafy vegetables, safflower and sunflower oils, foods low in saturated animal fats, fresh fruits, vegetables, pasta, and whole grain breads in your daily diet. Foods with natural and low sugar content will provide the energy that helps keep your brain cells in peak condition. When you consider these factors, it makes sense to eat a diet based on those foods that will optimize your energy.

Energy foods are not only good for us to eat, but are also the core foundations of our health and vitality. The daily amount of food each individual needs will vary depending on activity, age, and most importantly, the type of metabolism they have. When you consider these factors, it makes sense to eat a diet based on fresh fruits, vegetables, pasta, and whole grain breads to optimize your energy level.

Maximize the nutritional value of everything you eat to get the most out of life. Energy foods should be healthy, tasty, and colorful, and best of all - these foods can truly increase your quality of life. See for yourself.

## FRUITS AND VEGETABLES

Fresh fruits and vegetables contribute to good health and vitality for the human body. They are naturally high in fiber, low in cholesterol, as well as being rich in polyunsaturated fats and essential amino and fatty acids. Most of these natural foods are delicious, relatively inexpensive, and can be enjoyed raw or cooked at any time with minimum effort. Over-cooking fruits and vegetables can alter their chemical make up and destroy essential nutrients. Vitamins A, C, and E (which are important antioxidants), thiamin, and folic acid are damaged or destroyed by heat.

Have you ever wondered what makes organic fruits and vegetables different from the other fruits and vegetables you see in the produce department of your local supermarket? These fruits and vegetables are grown using traditional pesticide-free methods, with natural fertilizers containing more nutrients.

## CEREAL AND GRAINS

**Cereal and grains are the main sources of energy and protein.**

**Buckwheat** - has a traditional reputation for being 'warming and drying', provides a good source of energy in winter.

**Millet** - a good source of magnesium and iron, and makes a delicious alternative to oats in porridge.

**Oats** - a high protein cereal, rich in iron. It helps lower blood cholesterol levels, decreasing the risk of coronary heart disease.

**Rice** - a great source of protein, energy, fiber, and B-vitamins.

**Rye** - a great source of protein.

**Wheat** - a good source of carbohydrates. It is used to make bread, pasta, couscous, and tubule.

## PEAS, BEANS AND LENTILS

Peas, beans, and lentils are packed with protein, carbohydrates, fiber, vitamins, and minerals. They are extremely satisfying, and have minimal fat content. Also known as legumes, they have the ability to lower blood cholesterol and help prevent heart disease. Legumes have the ability to delay digestion and absorption, which makes for an ideal food for diabetics. Legumes are inexpensive, versatile, and easy to store.

## PASTA

Durum wheat (traditional pasta) is particularly high in protein gluten, which makes it easy to form into various shapes (spaghetti, lasagna, penne, macaroni, fettuccine, etc.). Durum wheat is digested more slowly than other wheat products, releasing a steady flow of energy into the body.
Whole grain pasta (durum wheat), when mixed with other wheat flour, is richer in vitamins, and heavier in texture than other pasta.

## BREADS

Breads are rich in protein, fiber, B-vitamins, iron, calcium, and trace elements. Breads can be made from any cereal, but wheat flour is recommended. Eating whole grain breads helps contribute to long-term health, and adds flavor and substance to the diet.
Food for thought: In order to build a durable house (your body), you need to build a strong foundation.


*MORE NUTRITION TIPS AND BITS*


## RECOMMENDED SERVING SIZES AND SERVING PORTIONS

Bread, cereal, rice, and pasta: the recommended daily servings are 6 to 11.
1 slice or 1-ounce wheat bread
½ cup cooked cereal
1-ounce cold cereal
½ cup cooked pasta or rice (whole wheat pasta or brown rice is recommended)

Fruits: the recommended daily servings are 2 to 5.
1 fruit
1 melon wedge
½ cup canned fruit

¾ cup fruit juice
¼ cup dried fruit

Low-fat milk, yogurt and cheeses: the recommended daily servings are 2 to 3.
1 cup milk or yogurt
1.5 ounces of cheese

Meat, poultry, fish, eggs, dry beans nuts: the recommended daily servings are 2 to 3.
2 to 3 ounces cooked lean meat, poultry, or fish
1 egg
1½ cup cooked beans

Vegetables: the recommended daily servings are 3 to 5.
½ cup raw or cooked vegetables
1 cup leafy vegetables

## DID YOU KNOW...

- one gram of protein has four calories?

- one gram of fat has nine calories?

- one gram of carbohydrates has four calories?

- one gram of alcohol has seven calories?

## DAILY FAT INTAKE - Recommended Daily Allowance (RDA)

Daily Calorie Diet

1200 Calories
RDA- less than 40 grams

1500 Calories
RDA -less than 50 grams

2000 Calories
RDA - less than 65 grams

2500 Calories
RDA - less than 80 grams

3000 Calories
RDA- less than 100 grams

3500 Calories
RDA- less than 115 grams

4000 Calories
RDA- less than 130 grams

4500 Calories
RDA- less than 150 grams

5000 Calories
RDA- less than 165 grams

The average American eats about 85 grams of fat a day, which adds up to 765 calories (assuming you are consuming 2000 calories a day). That 85 grams of fat is equivalent to 38% of your total daily caloric intake. If you are a frequent patron at fast food establishments, it is quite possible to eat 85 grams in one sitting.

DAILY CARBOHYDRATE INTAKE * - Recommended Daily Allowance (RDA)
* Represents approximately 60 % of total calories

Daily Calorie Diet
1200 Calories
RDA-180 grams

1500 Calories
RDA- 225 grams

2000 Calories
RDA- 300 grams

2500 Calories
RDA-375 grams

3000 Calories
RDA - 450 grams

3500 Calories
RDA- 525 grams

4000 Calories
RDA- 600 grams

4500 Calories
RDA- 675 grams

5000 Calories
RDA -750 grams

## DAILY CALCIUM INTAKE - Recommended Daily Allowance (RDA)

## Age Group

Young children through teens
RDA- 1300 milligrams

Adults
RDA-1000 milligrams

Mature adults 50 years and older
RDA- 1200 milligrams

## DAILY SODIUM INTAKE

No more than 2000/milligrams a day is the recommended daily allowance.

More than 55 million Americans, or 1 out of every 4, have hypertension (high blood pressure), which is a major cause for heart disease, stroke, and sometimes heart failure. Sodium is also associated with hypertension, but not everybody is salt-sensitive, and the reduction of salt intake does not always lead to lower blood pressure. Some of the risk factors include poor diet, obesity, high stress, and smoking. Eating a healthier than average diet and exercising on a regular basis will help eliminate some of these risk factors.

## DAILY CALORIE INTAKE TO MAINTAIN YOUR CURRENT WEIGHT

The following formulas will help you determine the number of calories needed daily to maintain your current weight: choose which lifestyle you have and then multiply your weight by the number given: this will give you the number of daily calories needed for weight maintenance.

**Determining Your Calorie Intake:**

To determine the number of calories you will need to maintain your current weight, follow these guidelines:

If your lifestyle is:

- **SENDATARY**

Formula: Your current weight_____ multiplied by 13 = _____ (Your total represents the number of calories that you will need to eat to maintain your current weight.)

- **MODERATELY ACTIVE**

Formula: Your current weight_____ multiplied by 14 = _____ (Your total represents the number of calories that you will need to eat to maintain your current weight.)

- **ACTIVE**

Formula: Your current weight_____ multiplied by 15 = _____ (Your total represents the number of calories that you will need to eat to maintain your current weight.)

- **ATHLETIC**

Formula: Your current weight_____ multiplied by 16 = _____ (Your total represents the number of calories that you will need to eat to maintain your current weight.)

## GUIDELINES FOR GAINING OR LOSING WEIGHT

**Guidelines for gaining and losing weight:**

- To gain one pound a week, you need to increase your caloric intake by 3500 calories a week (500 calories a day)

- To lose one pound a week, you need to reduce your calorie intake by 3500 calories a week (500 calories a day).

**It is not as hard to do as it sounds to lose or maintain your weight. That donut you ate this morning may contain as many as 200 calories...ouch! That adds up to an extra 1400 calories a week, or 20 pounds a year. Here's another startling fact - eating just ½ cup of ice cream a day, which may have 150 calories, adds up to 1050 calories a week, or 15 pounds a year.**

# PART V

## *WEIGHT LOSS*
༄*

## *MIRACLE DIETS & GADGETS*

Americans spend more than $40 billion every year trying to get a handle on managing their weight. Some people have success, while others see the excess weight they lost quickly return. Many even return to their original weight shortly after their weight loss program ends, possibly continuing to gain more and more weight. It is not unusual to go back to old eating patterns once one goes off their weight loss program. Promises, Promises, Promises. Infomercials say you can lose 20 pounds in two weeks on a juice diet; lose weight while you sleep; use exercise gizmos to trim your waist, and remove cellulite, etc. As the old saying goes "if it sounds too good to be true, it probably is too good to be true."

There is so much misinformation and misconception about weight loss products that an enormous number of desperate people have been scammed and ripped off, all for the sake of trying to lose a few pounds. It seems like everyone is looking for the magic formula to shed pounds, but unfortunately, some people become victims of weight loss fraud. The misleading claims by these companies have become so rampant the Federal Drug Enforcement Agency has begun to monitor them more closely.

Whether you are reading a magazine, watching television, or listening to a friend sing the praises of the latest diet, advertisements are everywhere pushing weight loss pills, patches, liquids, or exercise gadgets to help you get rid of extra weight. Sure, some of these products may give you temporary weight loss, but why pay for temporary satisfaction when you can have a permanent and healthier life by cutting back on calories and fat grams?

Weight loss has very little to do with celebrity diets, abdominal machines, and late night infomercials promising instant weight loss (lose thirty pounds in thirty days, etc.). You lose weight on almost any diet at first, because when you start a new weight loss program, you most likely eat less food than your body is accustomed to consuming.

After following a diet successfully for a while, the body senses it is not receiving adequate amounts of food, so goes into a state of deprivation. Once you begin to eat somewhat regularly again, the fat cells in the body awaken and absorbs the food, like a sponge absorbs water. It gets worse - the body then begins to store fat in reserve, preparing for the next starvation period. This cycle will start all over again when the next new diet fad arrives: a never-ending process.

Losing weight is only half the battle: the challenge is keeping it off. My goal is to inform and educate readers about the importance of making long-term lifestyle changes, instead of utilizing quick-fix fad diets. It will take hard work, persistence, and dedication to get one's body in the physical shape desired. One can take many short cuts to lose weight rapidly, but a long-term commitment to healthier eating and using a regular exercise program will give one a greater sense of accomplishment.

A few words about 'spot reducing'. There is no such thing as spot reducing on the body. There is a myth that if you do stomach crunches you can get a flat stomach with rippling muscles. In reality, abdominal exercises can only strengthen abdominal muscles. Core exercises are best if you are trying to strengthen your lower back as well as flatten your stomach. The best way to lose fat mass around your waistline is to follow a sensible diet and exercise regularly.

Some of the claims on advertised cellulite products promise to eliminate cellulite by increasing blood circulation and reducing localized fats, thus freeing trapped fat. (Cellulite is the cottage cheese-looking, puckered fat that forms on hips, buttocks, and thighs.) In reality, you reduce cellulite as you would any fat, by adjusting your diet and engaging in regular exercise. However, for some people cellulite is genetic, and a fact of life for them. There are other options available for reducing cellulite, but you should get those recommendations from your doctor.

Motivation to workout comes naturally for some people; for the rest of us, inspiration to exercise is a hard thing to maintain. There are also many diets, but making a lifestyle change will get you off to a great start to a healthier you.

Note: Diets that eliminate important food groups do not work. Food restriction often leaves you hungry, and eventually you will give up on your diet program and start eating unhealthy foods again.

## WEIGHT LOSS PLATEAUS

When your weight loss hits a plateau or comes to a standstill, it's the body's way of telling you that it is preparing itself for a period of famine. It is not getting the quantity of food that it is used to, so the body is lowering its metabolism in an attempt to slow the use its of fatty reserves.

In the early stages of any weight loss program, the weight will drop off quickly; in some cases as much as 5 pounds the first week. Most of the weight loss is water and carbohydrates. As a person begins to eat less, their body begins to burn stored fat and carbohydrates for energy. The longer the diet is maintained, and the same level of exercise continued, the body will begin to acclimate to this temporary regiment. Unfortunately, a time will come when the rate of loss will slow to what may be considered a snail's pace. This is commonly known as a plateau.

To break this aggravating standstill, you will need to adjust your calorie intake for further weight loss. Increase your physical activity so that you are burning 250 to 500 more calories a day, and simultaneously reduce your caloric intake by 250 to 500 calories to jump-start your weight loss again. However, calorie cutting can also create an adverse reaction and keep you from losing weight because of the effect it has on your metabolism.

Unless you are under a doctor's supervision, you should never drop your daily caloric intake below 1200; you will struggle to shed excess pounds, and put your health at risk.

If you want to get off your weight loss plateau, you will need to shake up your metabolism: Here are a few recommendations to help you rattle your metabolism and get you started again:

- Try not to skip meals. You will end up eating more food than if you had eaten a regular meal.

- Try to change your eating patterns. If you are not quite sure how to track what foods you are eating, keep a daily food journal to stay aware of the foods, and the amount of food that you eat.

- Change your fitness program. Once the muscles get acclimated to the same, repetitious movements, they become complacent. Changing your fitness routine, no matter how much you may like it, will help your body start to burn more calories.

- Your chances of getting off the plateau increase if you change your fitness routine often, as the new muscles you are beginning to work hard helps increase the number of calories that you burn.

- If you are working out 3 days a week doing a cardiovascular activity, change your program to include cross training activities (calisthenics, cardio, strength training, and a core exercise).

When eating a meal, focus on your food. Eliminate distractions like television or reading, and never eat while you are driving.

Losing weight is influenced by more than calories in and calories out. The energy it takes to keep your heart beating, lungs breathing, and other body systems working is known as your basal metabolic rate. It can be measured after a person has not eaten or moved for at least 12 hours.

Your resting metabolic rate includes the basal metabolic rate, plus the additional energy required for being awake, alert, and sitting up. Your resting metabolic rate accounts for 60% to 70% of the energy you expend daily. Your resting metabolic rate is closely linked to how much lean muscle mass you have: the more lean muscle mass you have, the higher your resting metabolic rate.

## *DINING OUT - PLANNING YOUR STRATEGY*

Nearly everyone likes to dine out at restaurants, and, some of us dine out more than others. Due to busy schedules, many people have very little time to prepare three meals a day for their families. Restaurant dining offers an opportunity for us to be pampered, and served foods prepared by someone else.

The heavy competition in the restaurant industry is often quite fierce, with each restaurant doing what it can to entice diners to their establishments. Some restaurants are well known for serving 'super-sized portions' or heavy cholesterol on a plate (fried foods), and most of us are quite aware of at least one or two eating establishments that do this, so we keep going back for more regularly.

Restaurant dining offers many wonderful, versatile menu selections. Sometimes the healthy choice may not be as obvious as the fattening selections on the menu. However, upon close inspection, one can always find something on the menu that will accommodate their culinary tastes. It is very important to incorporate 'dining out' into a weight loss program to avoid a temporary relapse of unhealthy eating.

The secret to successful dining away from home is your 'planning strategy'.
If you *plan* to order a healthy, low-fat meal, you can follow through with it.

**Here are few techniques that always work for me:**

**Have a small, low-fat snack before going to the restaurant**. Forget about ruining your appetite because you are eating a snack to take the edge off your hunger pangs. This will help prevent you from overindulging once you get to the restaurant. A few suggestions for a 'before meal' snack are lite crackers, low-fat cheese, yogurt, veggie sticks, and green salad with low calorie dressing. Eating before you leave home helps you make better, rational decisions when ordering your food.

**Wear something that is form fitting,** as it will help remind you why you are practicing portion control. Wearing clothing that fits you snugly also helps focus your attention away from ordering foods that would be detrimental to your body and how you want to look.

**If you have tried the previous two suggestions** and still managed to overeat, the next best strategy is to exercise to help melt away some of those extra calories. If you exercise moderately before dining out, you will accomplish two things: a decreased appetite, and remembering your workout efforts will provide incentive not to overdo it at the restaurant.

## MAKING GOOD FOOD CHOICES

Although restaurants offer fattening dishes, some are slowly becoming more sensitive and responsive to the growing request for low-fat, low calorie meals. These restaurant owners are adjusting their menus to meet the new dietary trends.

I have found that restaurants catering to business people who dine out often are starting to add 'cholesterol free', 'smart start', and more weight watcher type foods to their menus. These meals are usually prepared with fewer saturated fats, less sugar, lower sodium, and more fruits and veggies. Try venturing away from your regular dining spots until you find restaurants that serve foods like whole grain breads, brown rice, fat-trimmed meats, choices of fresh fruits, lightly cooked appetizers, vegetable and bean soups. (These soups are great because they are filling, but offer fewer calories).

Customize your food order to correspond to your style of healthy eating. Order gravies and sauces on the side, and dip your food; this will give you more control over the calories. Remember that you do not have to eat everything on the plate because you purchased it. Stop eating when you have had enough food. If you are not sure, push the plate towards the center of the table and wait twenty minutes. Usually, before the twenty minutes have passed you will realize that you no longer have a desire to eat more food at this sitting.

**Listed below are some of the safe food picks that are served by a variety of ethnic eateries:**

**Mexican Food**: Chicken fajitas and chicken burritos. Use salsa; skip the guacamole and sour cream.

**Fast Foods**: Salad with low-fat dressings, grilled chicken, a small burger without sauce.

**Deli Foods**: Turkey breast or lean roast beef sandwich with mustard on wheat bread.

**Italian Food**: Spaghetti served with red or white clam sauce.

**Chinese Food**: Szechwan shrimp, stir fried vegetables, shrimp in garlic sauce, chicken chow mein (request that these dishes be prepared with minimal oil).

**Pizzerias**: Pizza with vegetable toppings instead of pepperoni, sausage, extra cheese, or the deep-dish version. Try the hand tossed crust, it's usually thinner and has less calories.

## *KNOW THE RESTAURANT LINGO*

There are particular words listed on the menu that should be seen as RED FLAGS. I cannot mention them all, but here are a few words that you may not be aware of, but need to know: Alfredo, au gratin, breaded, butter sauce, buttery, cheese sauce, cream sauce, creamy, dipped in butter, glazed, hollandaise, pan fried, piled high (or stacked), sautéed, scalloped, or stuffed with meat or cheese.

You get the picture. Okay, you are probably wondering what is left to eat? Plenty.

**Here is a list of words describing healthily prepared foods to eat: baked, braised, broiled, garden fresh, in broth, in its own juice, marinara (tomato sauce), pickled, poached, primavera (with vegetables), roasted, steamed, stewed, and stuffed with vegetables or herbs.**

You see, there are plenty of options. You have almost made it!

When your food arrives at the table, assess your order, and make sure that you received baked instead of fried. Is your side order just that - on the side of the plate, or has it been poured on top of your plate? If your order is not up to your request, do not be bashful but politely alert your food server. After all, you have made it this far in your dining experience without incident, why sabotage your endeavors now?

Finally, drink plenty of water throughout the meal and you will eat less. Concentrate on enjoying conversation with your meal companion, and enjoy your meal…. you have earned it!

## MORE WEIGHT LOSS TIPS

- Avoid foods high in saturated fats.

- Avoid processed foods, overly ripe foods, and over-cooked foods.

- Do not go on diet extremes, i.e., eating all protein foods, all fruit, all soup, etc.

- Drink an 8-ounce glass of water before eating your meal.

- Eat a diet of five or more servings of fruits daily.

- Eat foods that are low on the Glycemic Index.

- Eat fresh vegetables that are either raw or lightly steamed to preserve the nutrients.

- Eat more fruits, vegetables, and whole grains.

- Eat your evening meal 3 hours prior to your bedtime.

- Exercise at least five times a week for weight loss.

- Have reasonable weight loss expectations.

- Increase your daily protein intake. (Without protein, your body cannot build muscle.)

- Keep a food/mood journal.

- Learn to meditate to help relieve stress.

- Eat your last meal of the day three hours before bedtime.

- Marinate your fish or chicken to create more flavors before baking or grilling.

- Never skip meals.

- Take vitamin and mineral supplements.

- Try to eat as many whole-grain products as possible.

- Use a non-stick spray in your cooking pan.

- Use fresh herbs like dill, garlic, bay leaf, parsley, basil, etc., to flavor foods.

- When dining out, order salad dressing and other condiments in separate dishes on the side.

## YOU ARE ON YOUR WAY TO A HEALTHY LIFESTYLE!

## SOURCES, RESOURCES, AND SUGGESTED READING

American Heart Lung and Blood Institute
www.afpafitness.com/articles
www.bodybuildingforyou.com/articles
www.caloriesperhour.com
www.dietandbody.com
www.doctoryourself.com
www.ehow.com/how
www.epa.gov/safewater/dwhealth.html
www.exrx.net/exercise.html
www.fitnessjournal.org
www.ga.water.usga.gov
www.gmhc.org/health/nutrition/liver/detox
www.healthcastle.com/high-fiber-foods.shtml
www.healthypages.net
www.heartofpilates.com
www.hsph.harvard.edu/nutritionsource/carbohydrates.html
www.infobeagle
www.intenseworkout.com/protein_diet.html
www.itms.ecol.net/fitness/strindex
www.jhbmc.jhu/edu/cariology/rehab/fiber
www.medical.webends.com/kw/somatotypes
www.mindbodyyoga.com
www.moderateindependent.com
www.physportsmed.com/issues
www.primusweb.com/fitnesspartner/jumpsite
www.realtime.net/anr/nutrient.html
www.sportsmedicine.about.com/cs
www.strengthfit.com
www.surgeongeneral.gov
www.thefruitpages.com
www.Tunu.com
www.uh.edu/fitness/community%20Educators.com
www.vitamins-nutrition.org
www.weightlossforall.com/body-types-weig
www.weightlossforgood.ca.uk/exercise

## SUGGESTED READING

Women's Strength Training Anatomy-Frederic Delavier
The New Fit or Fat- Covert Bailey
Yoganetics- Wyatt Townley
Power Foods- Liz Applegate, Ph.D.
Pilates Basics- Jillian Hessel
If Its Not Food ...Don't Eat It- Kelly Hayford
Yoga For Beginners-Mark Ansari and Liz Lark
The Mind-Body Makeover Project- Michael Gerrish
Fit for Life- Harvey and Marilyn Diamond
Fast Food Nation-Eric Schlosser
The Fat Burning Bible- Mackie Shilstone
Strong Women Stay Young- Miriam E. Nelson, Ph.D.
Body, Mind and Sport-Douillard
The Complete Book of Stretching- Tony Lycholat

## *STARR'S FAVORITE QUOTES*

It is here, my daughters, that love is to be found - not hidden away in the corners but in the midst of occasions of sin. And believe me, although we may more often fail and commit small lapses, our gain will be incomparably the greater.

Saint Teresa of Avila

The quality of our laughter and joy, the knowledge of our voices, thoughts and actions are weaving beauty around the land.

Dhyani Ywahoo

Always we must come around the circle to find the harmony in ourselves. It is never really lost; we have only to accept it and let ourselves resonate with the whole universe.

Dhyani Ywahoo

Anything we do is an alone journey. No matter how happy your friends may be for you, how much they support you, you can't expect anyone to match the intensity of your emotions or to completely understand what you went through.

Natalie Goldberg

Whoever you are, whatever you are, start with that, whether salt of the earth or only white sugar.

Alice Walker

Compassion literally means to feel with, to suffer with. Everyone is capable of compassion, and yet everyone tends to avoid it because it's uncomfortable. And the avoidance produces psychic numbing - resistance to experiencing our pain for the world and other beings.

Joanna Macy

Life is playfulness...we need to play so that we can rediscover the magic all around us.

Flora Colao

If you know you are not your sports car, your grades or your children's grades, your color, your degrees, your spouse's degrees, your age, your titles or your family's title, your body, your possessions or your parent's possessions - Congratulations. You are home again.

Rusty Berkus

If you give your life as a prayer you intensify the prayer beyond all measure. To attain inner peace you must actually give your life, not just your possessions. When you give your life bringing into alignment your beliefs and the way you live, then and only then, can you begin to find inner peace.

Peace Pilgrim

Remember that you are this universe and that this universe is you - remember that all is in motion, in growing, is you.

Joy Harjo

Let us be clear that when I say Goddess I am not talking about a being somewhere outside of the world, nor am I proposing a new belief system. I am talking about choosing an attitude: choosing to take the living world, the people and creatures on it, as the ultimate meaning and purpose of life, to see the world, the earth, and our lives as sacred.

Starhawk

But we have been ripening to a greater ease, learning to accept, that all hungers cannot be fed. That saving the world, may be a matter of sowing a seed, not overturning a tyrant. That we do what we can.

Mary Sarton

My feeling is, the better we feel about ourselves, the fewer times we have to knock somebody down in order to stand on top of their bodies and feel tall.

Odetta

Beauty and grace are performed whether or not we will sense them. The least we can try to do is be there.

Annie Dillard

We can do anything we want to do, if we stick to it long enough.

Helen Keller

Don't live for the present: don't allow transitory things to influence you. Live in eternity, above time and space, above finite things. Then nothing can influence you.

Elisabeth Haich

Human beings are set apart from the animals. We have a spiritual self, a physical self and a consciousness. Therefore we can make choices and are responsible for the choices we make. We may choose order and peace or confusion and chaos.

Rosa Parks

We need to retain an open heart so that whatever or whenever we do anything our action will be an act of love and compassion and nothing less.

Dr. Thynn Thynn

I weep a lot. I thank God, I laugh a lot too. The main thing in one's own private world is to try to laugh as much as you cry.

Maya Angelou

When we understand how precious each moment, we can treat each breath, each moment as a newborn baby. Awareness can become that tender.

Michele McDonald

I long to accomplish a great and noble task, but it is my chief duty to accomplish small tasks as if they were great and noble.

Helen Keller

To succeed, jump as quickly at opportunities, as you do at conclusions.

Benjamin Franklin

The secret of success is to be ready when your opportunity comes.

Benjamin Disraeli

Problems are opportunities in work clothes.

Henry J. Kaiser

320484